ENTREPRENE

GET A KLU

IN 52

Soft Skills for Strong Leaders

Jeffrey Klubeck
Vipul Dayal

Get a Klu in 52

Entrepreneur Edition

Soft Skills for Strong Leaders

Jeffrey Klubeck and Vipul Dayal

Cover design by Sean O'Connor
OhSeeDesign@gmail.com

Editing, typography, and layout by Patti McKenna
Pattimck6@gmail.com

Printed in the United States of America

TABLE OF TIPS

PERSONAL BRANDING

T I P #1

BRANDING IS **NOT** A SPECTATOR SPORT

 When it comes to branding, be very clear that it is an ACTIVE, never passive, phenomenon. Something that we will repeat over and over and over again in the tips in this section and the book overall is that a brand is a promise to the marketplace … and YOUR brand is YOUR promise to the marketplace.

So, get this: Even if you *decided* you did not need a personal brand and *declared* that you do not even know what your personal brand is, let alone what it should be, and *believed* or even *intended* that you have NO personal brand, you'd still have a personal brand! ☺

Let me elaborate using two truths I taught my Communication students as a college professor:

1) Communication is RECEIVER based! By this, we are referring to the "decoding" process when an "observer" (receiver) makes meaning of what they observe/receive. We all make meaning of anything we pay attention to … in fact, nothing is really a "message" until we pay attention to it and decide what it means. Until then, it's just piece of stimuli—a sound, sight, touch, taste, or odor—whether that "thing" had any intention of being observed or not! That leads to the second truth:

2) Non-verbal communication can be both intentional and UN-intentional! Very often, we intend to "send" non-verbal messages … non-verbal being EVERYTHING other than words/linguistics that can

be observed and "decoded" into meaning. Intentional communication is when a source/sender "encodes" their intentions into something observable that then gets "decoded" when observed. We do that intentionally a LOT. In fact, we are a "source" of non-verbal communication as long as we are observable! Because 100% of the time that ANYONE can observe us, they can make any meaning they want of whatever they observe.

Combine these two truths and we realize that regardless of what we intend or believe or declare or decide, the "marketplace" is always deciding for itself what things mean.

It is easy to underestimate the importance of personal branding and avoid actively participating in your brand. The truth, however, is that branding occurs whether you participate in it or not. If you do not take the time to brand yourself, the market will brand you, and it may not do it favorably. Customers can bring negative attention to a company or individual, and attention can easily escalate to the court of public opinion. Taking control of personal branding is necessary to manage your public reputation.

Observers will always make their own meaning of what they observe unless we proactively do the work of ensuring they'll make the meaning we want made. That is not always 100% possible, however failing to proactively develop, promote, and deliver on our brand promise leaves "what people can expect from us" up to THEM!

What we want you to get from this tip is to take branding seriously and know that you are branding yourself 100 percent of the time, simply because one way or another, people will come to learn what they can expect from you. We want you to be ON TOP of that messaging ... to control that narrative ... to prioritize developing the promises you know you can consistently make and deliver to the marketplace ... to be proactive and consistent about your commitment to making sure people KNOW exactly what they can expect from you!

T I P #2

BE THE PROMISE

If you chose to be proactive after reading Tip #1, you are in control of your personal brand. Now, you are ready to begin the "how to" of personal branding. As we mentioned in Tip #1, a brand is a promise to the marketplace, and a personal brand is a promise to BE the promise.

A great promise is only partly about you as we'll discuss below. First, we must make sure you know that a promise cannot be great unless it is one that your customers care about. Meaning, a "marketable" promise is one that gets people away from pain or closer to pleasure (or both). Pleasure and pain are the two primary motivators of all human behavior. So, a promise that will catch the attention of your potential customers is a promise that relieves/eliminates pain or provides/ increases pleasure ... for THEM!

You have to imagine your customers, what they go through, what they say to themselves, what hardships they face, ...what accomplishments or lifestyle they desire. You have to be "biographical," instead of "auto-biographical," when imagining the promises you wish to make to the marketplace.

Coming up with brand promises is harder than it may seem, and we really want you to consider us approachable if you need help brainstorming, sound-boarding, and refining specific brand promises you can be confident making.

Meanwhile, it is HOW you make and follow through on those promises that IS totally about you!

Your brand is not just "marketing messaging." Your brand will be something that you will need to BE! Your behaviors will have to represent and be consistent with the branding you've put out to the marketplace.

Remember that perception is reality, so it is essential that you carefully cultivate your image. When you take the time to define yourself and present this definition to the public, your will benefit from the hard work of knowing who you really are and who you can really BE on a daily/hourly/minute-by-minute basis ... because who you *really are* is usually what the real b*rand really is*!

Be Real

First and foremost, you'll need to "keep it real!" People are attracted to genuine people. The key to personal branding is to make it personal. Communicating dry facts will not impress most people. Your brand must have personality. Develop a persona that attracts people. Share ideas, implement humor, and make connections with people. Having an online presence makes sharing your persona much easier.

While you need to remember to be real, you are under no obligation to share personal details about yourself, but everything that you do share must be genuine. Never make up facts, statistics, or tell lies. Fact checking has become easier than ever, and lies will do nothing to improve your brand's reputation.

Be Vulnerable

Being real is about being truthful to what is known. Being "vulnerable," however, is the effort to learn more about what is true ... to look further within for additional important truths that may not yet be known.

In very simple terms, we'd recommend a SWOT Analysis:

By identifying your *strengths, weaknesses, opportunities, and threats*, you will be able to define your brand and understand what you have to offer. You will also identify areas that need improvement.

- **Strengths**: Strengths are internal characteristics that create a competitive advantage. For example, accounting skills would be a strength.

- **Weaknesses**: Internal weaknesses that need to be improved. Disorganization would be an example of a weakness.

- **Opportunities**: Opportunities are external. There are always opportunities for you to take advantage of in the marketplace. Education would be an example of an opportunity.

- **Threats**: External threats cannot be controlled, but they may be addressed in your opportunities. Competition with a more relevant skill set is a threat.

A SWOT analysis will be unique to each person or business. Taking a moment to honestly assess your situation will allow you to complete a personal SWOT analysis and help understand which day-to-day behaviors will come naturally in support of your brand and which behaviors will represent more challenge.

Vipul and I love integrating Behavioral Assessments such as DISC & Motivators in the process of facilitating leaders, teams, and organizations in SWOT Analysis! Contact us to learn more about our Assessment and Team Building packages!

T I P #3

GET UP, STAND UP!

The best way to "Be Your Brand" day in and day out is to know (or discover/declare) what you "get up for" and what you "stand for!" Passions are what get you up! They "get you out of bed or off the couch," as I like to say. Meanwhile, Pillars are what "hold up" the promises/ offerings of your brand and business. Remember, your brand promise to the marketing place is what they will "get," while your passions and pillars represent how you will deliver on the promise!

Passions

Your brand should reflect your passions. Ask yourself the following questions to identify your passions:

- What do you care about?
- What drives you?
- What do you consider your passions?

Remember to list all of your passions, not just those that are obviously related to work. If the only passion you communicate is the desire to increase sales, you'll appear boring and work obsessed. People know that there is more to you than your work. Your brand needs to personalize you to other people, so a passion for art, family, or the environment could only contribute to your brand. You are bound to attract people with similar passions. You can also find ways to incorporate your passions into your work.

People who know me are well aware of my passion for baseball and attending live sporting events. Vipul and I both share a passion for playing golf, and Vipul is also passionate about volleyball and cars, to name a few. We both find ways to incorporate our passions into our businesses through networking events, investments, volunteerism, or sponsorships.

Pillars

 In branding, your pillars are your main values. They are the attributes that help define your identity. In order to identify your pillars, you must ask yourself what you stand for and what your core values are. Your pillars are not what you have to offer; they explain *how* you offer what you have. For example, you may offer years of sales experience, but your pillar could be offering an honest and authentic sales experience. Remember that there are no correct or incorrect pillars; they simply need to reflect your core values.

Ask yourself what you stand for and make a list of ideas. Then, choose the main values and link them to what your brand has to offer. It is best to begin branding with one or two pillars. You can always expand in the future but start out by trying to make a list of ten main values … ten things you want to be known for upholding or being upheld by (faith, trust, efficiency, loyalty, service, variety, fun, etc.). After you have ten, find the two that mean more to you than all of the other eight combined. We are willing to bet those are your pillars!

Vipul and I love working with entrepreneurs/owners to determine, among the hundreds of choices, which noble values among them will be declared as Pillars of the brand and business!

T I P #4

IDENTIFICATION = (AND EQUALS) DIFFERENTIATION!

Thank you for tolerating the title of this tip! We are being intentionally contradictory when saying that "Identification" both equals and fails to equal "Differentiation!" This is because the "laws of physics" are different than the "rules of marketing!"

In physics, your fingerprint is enough to identify you, because we all know that no two sets of fingerprints are the same. By definition, according to the laws of physics, your identification is what technically separates you from other people ... literally by definition, unique equals different.

KLOOBY SNACK

The "laws of physics" are different than the "rules of marketing!"

In marketing, however, being "unique" alone is not enough to establish the "differentiation" we need!

Unless you are the only game in town, the rules of marketing require you to be "competitive" in order to have "differentiation." It isn't enough to simply ask potential customers to "tell you apart" from the competition when the success of your brand and business is to get potential customers to CHOOSE you from among your competition!

In Tip #2, the "S" in SWOT analysis asked you to get honest about all of your strengths and suggested that strengths create competitive advantages. But here in Tip #4, we need to go just a bit deeper.

Something you can expect us to repeat several times through this section (and this book as a whole) is: **You must answer two critical questions to know your competitive advantages:**

- Better! Of all the things that both you AND your competition do, which of them do you DO better? Of all the things both you and your competition have, which are "better" than what your competition has? Better pricing? Better service? Better quality? Better selection? Better convenience? Better experience? What is better and better, how?

- Different/Unique: Of all the people/businesses that compete with you, what do you HAVE or DO that they do not HAVE or DO? Again, a business name or Tax ID number is not enough to satisfy this question in this context.

In fact, both questions require you to answer from the perspective of the customer. Remember, your business has to deliver on that brand promise … or failure to deliver BECOMES the promise! So we recommend "knowing," "developing," and/or "promoting" as many competitive advantages as you possibly can in your marketing!

Beware! This tip is easier to understand than it is to implement. Again, you have to come up with as many answers as you possibly can to BOTH questions above, and you will have the ingredients you need for Tip #4!

I have personally helped dozens of entrepreneurs from 12 different countries establish personal and company brands by forcing them to get clear on their Promises and Competitive Advantages! I love this work mostly for the steps that come after the discovery of promises and advantages: sloganeering and wordsmithing!

T I P #5

MADE TO STICK!

 Now we are ready to recommend one of my favorite things to do for myself and others: wordsmithing and sloganeering as a means to come up with memorable ways to communicate the brand to the marketplace!

In Tip s#1, we advised you to be pro-active and take branding seriously! In Tip #2, we advised you to get "biographical" when imagining the promises you will make to others, as well as "auto-biographical" when exploring your authenticity and SWOT analysis. Tips #3 and #4 asked you to get clear on your pillars, passions, and differentiation (competitive advantages).

Now, you have LOTS of ingredients to play with when constructing phrases, taglines, SEO keywords, and mantras that communicate your brand in "memorable/engaging" ways. It's one thing to make a promise to the marketplace; it's another thing to make a promise that STICKS!

Be Brief!

All the homework we've suggested in Tips 1-4 must get "boiled down" into the shortest and sweetest offerings you can imagine. Brand mantras or taglines are short, but they are powerful. This short phrase or statement might only be three to five words, but these words define your brand. A mantra must explore the brand's points of difference or how the brand is unique, along with what the company represents. For example, look at Nike's *"Authentic Athletic Performance."*

In order to create a brand mantra, you must first identify what sets your brand apart and list your points of difference. Once the points of difference are identified, create a mantra that is simple, communicates, and inspires.

- **Simple**: The mantra should be short and to the point. Another key to remember is to eliminate the jargon that customers may not understand and replace the jargon with "simpler" language.
- **Communicate**: The mantra should define the purpose of the brand and what is unique about it. What are you offering, and why should people get it from you vs. others who also offer it?
- **Inspire**: The mantra should be significant. Again, the customer should get a sense of pain relief or pleasure from the brand promises.

Again, when sloganeering to create a mantra, tagline, product, or event name (or even the name of your business), you should begin with a word bank of promises, points of difference, purpose/mission of the business, pillars, and perhaps your passions.

> When Vipul and I do the live online reading of this tip, you will be able to ask me about dozens of examples of brand names I helped create for entrepreneurs. I might even screen share the list of over 275 domains that I own as a result of the wordsmithing/sloganeering creative branding processes we engage in.

T I P #6

WHEN HUMILITY IS HUMILIATING

 Tips 1-5 in this section are heavy, compared to the brevity we strive for here. Tip #6 cautions you to beware of the "dishonesty of humility!"

It's kinda like when I offer people peanuts when I am enjoying a bag at a ballgame. So many times, people will say "no," and I know they are only saying "no" to be polite ... or what they believe to be polite. Then, I tell them that they're trying to be polite, and I believe being polite is a form of dishonesty ... especially if the person really DOES want some peanuts and really would enjoy a little handful ... at a ballgame, of all places! ☺

The same thing is true when it comes to branding and humility—a ballgame is NOT the place to say no to a couple peanuts offered by a fellow fan—and branding is NOT the time to be humble!

If you have been proactive, serious, diligent, hardworking, perhaps even soul searching about your purpose, promises, passions, pillars, strengths, and advantages, you deserve to shout your brand from the tops of mountains!

Moreover, when you KNOW (and I mean absolutely KNOW) you can back up your promises and deliver what you say you will deliver, HOW you say you deliver it, you are making a big mistake in being "humble" about it. Your customers NEED you. The world NEEDS you! Let them know you're here!

I had a neighbor who was a real estate agent, but you'd have to talk with him to know it. He wasn't the agent that knocked on your door … or had a magnetic sign on his car … or left flyers on your doorstep. He didn't attend networking events, let alone speak at community events as a subject matter expert on trends affecting buyers/sellers in the community. Well, one day, another mutual neighbor had a sign in his lawn, and as we all went to our cars to leave for work, I watched in pain as I saw my agent neighbor confront my "seller" neighbor.

"How on earth could you live right across the street from me and have my competitor's sign in your lawn?!"

The seller simply replied, "I'm sorry, neighbor. I did not know you were a realtor," and got in his car and drove off matter of factly.

The realtor came back to his own car and within earshot of me, said, "Can you believe that guy has been living across the street from me for nine years and never took the time to learn that I am a realtor!"

Do I need to reprint what I said to him to finish this story? ☺

"Neighbor, the fact that he does not know you are a realtor is 100% your fault, not his."

Branding is NOT the time to be humble … and we hope you avoid the humiliation that a humble approach might cause you!

Instead, work hard to arrive at the place where you KNOW what you are promising, WHY you can promise with confidence, and THAT you can deliver on that promise with your advantages and values! Get there, then fearlessly and tirelessly let the world KNOW!

T I P #7

BRAND VS. BRANDING

Here is a tip that also appears in the Marketing Section of the first and second editions of *Get A Klu in 52*. And this tip could easily have been Tip #1 in this section, given how important the distinction is … we really want you to focus in and memorize the difference between "brand" and "branding."

Aside from the obvious that one is a noun and the other a verb, be clear that *a brand is "the message"* (your promise to the marketplace, remember?), *whereas brandING is the totality of action aimed at putting brand messages into the marketplace.*

If only for the time you will save in your meetings and dialogue with others about marketing, make sure you are all on the same page with your terminology. The brand is the promise. The branding is how the promise is sent/received in the marketplace.

> ## KLOOBY SNACK
> A brand is "the message," whereas brandING is the totality of action aimed at putting brand messages into the marketplace.

Further benefits from this tip include a healthy division of labor between your techies (who want to know the technology to get the message out) and the people who are more likely to be your wordsmiths and sloganeers (see tip #8).

Another reason to know the difference between brand and branding is so each gets its fair and undiluted share of attention. When you are asking your brain for the words to communicate a promise, it will produce different answers than it would if you asked it for the best channels across which to deliver that promise!

TIP #8

PLAY THE INTEGRITY GAME!

You are constantly presenting your brand to other people, both in your personal and professional life. It is important that you understand how your personal brand and your professional brand reflect each other. When you are able to integrate them successfully, you will be able to use your brand to further your personal and professional life.

Corporate and Personal Integration

It is easy to believe that your personal life is completely separate from your professional life. Your personal brand, however, will intersect with your corporate brand, and the values of each need to reflect each other.

Consider how the reputations of professionals are ruined by personal scandals. If your personal brand conflicts with your professional, distrust for both your personal and professional brand will develop.

While you should try to integrate your personal and professional brands at all times, you must be particularly careful in certain situations. Behavior at public events, for example, needs to reflect your brand.

Additionally, you should exercise restraint when using social media. No matter your privacy settings, nothing online is private. What you say on your personal Twitter account needs to positively reflect your company's brand and your personal brand. If you must vent your frustrations, do so in a private setting that will not reflect poorly on you.

They Will Influence Each Other

Your personal and professional brands will influence each other. We are used to stories of a personal brand affecting a professional brand.

There are, however, ways that your professional brand will influence your personal brand. While we are accustomed to stories of negative influence, it is important to remember that the influence may also be positive.

For example, a CEO who performs a charitable act at work would influence his personal brand. People would view the personal brand in a positive light.

You must be mindful of how each brand will draw influences from the other.

Be a Professional

When developing your personal and professional brands, it is important that you exhibit professionalism. Be a professional both in and out of the office. In order to behave professionally, you need to define professional behavior. Not everyone defines professionalism the same way.

Some people are more rigid in their views, and others are more relaxed. There are, however, a few different ways to behave professionally that most people would agree are professional.

Professional Behavior:

- Be dependable
- Be competent in your work
- Act with honesty and integrity
- Treat everyone with respect
- Be a positive example

This list is not inclusive, but it is a good starting point. By behaving professionally in your personal and professional life, you will help create a brand that is respected.

Build Rapport

Part of personal branding requires building a rapport. When you build a rapport with people, you have the chance to develop a cross promotion between your personal and professional life that will lead to opportunities as you show your brand to potential employers, employees, and customers.

How to Build Rapport:

- **Consider your appearance**: Dress professionally.
- **Find mutual interest**: Discover common ground.
- **Exhibit honesty**: Be truthful in your interactions.
- **Show empathy**: Connect with people on an emotional level.

In our Coaching and Leadership Training programs, Vipul and I go way deeper in teaching how to build rapport than what we have chosen to share above. None of these tips are intended to be comprehensive coverage of the subjects they touch upon. We would love to talk with you to see if you are great candidate for our deep-dive Leadership Training.

FINAL NOTE ON THIS TIP: Even though we teach these principles, skills, guidelines, and so forth, we are human! In the spirit of vulnerability, please join Vipul and I for our weekly tip reading for a very specific story about when my branding behavior was *not* integrated personally and professionally. We look forward to discussing personal/professional brand integration with you!

T I P #9

BRAND PERSONA!

Brands need personality. Fortunately, you have the perfect opportunity to develop your brand and personality. The traits that your brand exhibits are completely up to you. When you identify your unique values and boldly look outside the box, your brand can have clear personality.

Identify Your Unique Attributes

When branding personality traits, you need to identify what makes you unique. This could be anything. For example, you could identify your creativity, outgoing personality, confidence, courage, or curiosity.

Once you identify what makes you valuable, you will be able to communicate it to others. If you have any trouble identifying your unique values, ask your friends and family for their advice.

Be Bold

Branding personality traits requires you to be bold. You cannot be shy in your efforts to expand your brand. You need to engage people in your brand and inspire their confidence. An excellent way you can do this is to use powerful words to describe yourself.

Examples of powerful words:

- Accomplished
- Insightful
- Leader

- Successful
- Independent

Some people will struggle with being bold, but it is not negotiable. People who lack the confidence to be bold can benefit from following the "fake it till you make it" technique. There are also classes specifically geared to help introverts connect.

Think Outside the Box

Thinking outside the box can facilitate the successful use of personal branding. Thinking outside the box requires you to take risks to promote your brand. There are a few simple ways to help you think outside of the box with your branding:

- Focus what you are trying to express.
- Brainstorm unconventional ways to communicate your idea.
- Consider ways to implement your idea.

Once you have brainstormed ideas, narrow them down to your top choice.

Fail. Learn. Repeat.

You will face failure in life, and your personal branding is no exception. You need to practice the process of fail, learn, and repeat. When you face failure, take the opportunity to learn from your mistakes, which creates learning moments. Once you learn from your mistakes, you are less likely to repeat them. If you repeat this process each time you fail, you will continue to learn from your mistakes and create a stronger brand.

Vipul and I love discussing our brand personalities ... from "Serial Go-Giver" to "Get A Klu" and "The Integrity Game," we have very personal examples of infusing personality into our personal and professional brands. And we want to know your brand's personality! We hope you'll join the live online discussion following the reading of this tip in 2022!

T I P #10

BRANDING VIA SOCIAL MEDIA

There are two tips left in this section, but, still, congratulations are in order! You have done a lot of work up to this point if you have implemented all of our tips. The best part is you now have ALL the ingredients you need to create amazing "branding messages" that you can flood the marketplace with.

So, it's time for our final two tips: Strategic Social Media and Protect The Brand! Starting with social media, what follows is an overview of major considerations when it comes to branding. We do not claim to be experts in social media. However, we each have had enough success with it in our own lives and businesses that we wanted to provide an overview of best practices.

At the end of the day, both Vipul and I do a lot of our own social media, as well as invest thousands of dollars each year in professional help with your social media. Here is an overview of our VERY BASIC best practices:

Strategic Social Media

Social media is an excellent way to improve your brand's presence. You must, however, use social media correctly in order for it to be effective. It is not enough to simply have social media accounts. You need have a specific purpose for your accounts and monitor them closely. It is also imperative that you implement security as you promote your brand.

Needs Constant Monitoring

Social media requires constant monitoring. If you do not pay attention to your social media accounts, they won't do you any good. When using social media, open accounts that are relevant to you and your business. Keep in mind that it is difficult to juggle numerous social media accounts.

 Once you are actively using social media, be sure to check your accounts regularly. You can also implement different tools to track your social media presence, some are paid, while others are not. Google Alerts is one useful tool you can use to monitor your social media accounts.

Free Tracking Tools:

- Hootsuite
- Viralheat
- Trendrr

Security

Everyone with an online presence needs to focus on Internet security. Being secure while using social media requires more than virus software. You need to use all of the security tools available to you, such as secure passwords and two-factor authentications or a two-step verification process.

Using two-factor authentications will keep your password safe. In this process, you enter your password, and a verification code is sent to your phone. The account cannot be accessed without the code.

To save time, you can establish it so that the code is not needed to log in on your home computer. Since the code is needed for other locations, it becomes more difficult to hack the account.

Choosing secure passwords and using different passwords for each account will improve security. A secure password is typically 8 to 10 characters and includes all of the following:

- Uppercase letters
- Lowercase letters
- Numbers
- Symbols or characters

Have an Objective

People who fail or are not completely successful using social media often only use it for general self-promotion. While social media is great for self-promotion, you need to have a clear objective in what you are promoting and how you promote it. Why are you there? What are you trying to promote? How does it translate to your brand?

For example, if you are passionate about fair trade, share your experiences and link to other articles, blogs, etc. Having an objective helps you to establish a network of followers with similar ideas.

Promote

Promoting your social media sites takes time and effort. There are many ways that you can increase the visibility of your brand using social media. The first step is to create the same message and theme throughout all of your social media sites' your Tumblr and your Facebook accounts should not share conflicting information; they should promote each other.

Certain tools allow you to link the same post to multiple sites. They should also have a similar look, color scheme, and feel to them.

You need to drive awareness of your brand by attracting people to you. The more connections you make, the more exposure you have. Don't be afraid to include links in your content.

Additionally, SEO can be implemented to improve your visibility. Find useful search terms and integrate them into your content to increase your search rankings. Running an SEO campaign is more complex than this, but choosing useful keywords is an excellent starting point.

It's a Tool

Social media may seem like a way of life, but it is a tool. Like any other tool, there is a learning curve. In order to use social media effectively, you need to practice. Experiment with different styles of communication until you find the one that best reflects your brand. Get feedback from your friends and improve with every entry or share.

Social Media Tips:

- Clearly establish what you want to communicate.
- Use attention-grabbing vocabulary.
- Use stories to engage people.
- Encourage readers to take action.

Content is King

Everyone is familiar with the phrase "content is king." It is not enough to simply create content; you have to make sure that it is good content. Your content needs to have a clear point that is relevant to your brand. Once you find a relevant topic, you have to communicate your opinions well.

How to Create Content:

- **Be relevant**: Stay informed on the latest trends that affect your brand. Writing about an old story is not likely to engage an audience.

- **Use variety:** Use both written and video content. Not everyone is skilled at writing.

- **Communicate well**: Make sure your written content is well written and factual. Make sure videos are edited properly.

Have a Gimmick

Almost everyone has a social media account, so that is not enough to set you apart. A useful way to stand out is to create a gimmick. *Gimmicks are not for everyone. If you do not want to use gimmicks, it is better to leave them alone. Better no gimmick than a poorly executed one.*

A gimmick is often a trick or some type of device to catch attention. You typically see it in advertising. Your brand will determine the type of gimmick that would work best for you.

Types of Gimmicks:

- Humorous
- Generous (give away)
- Create mystery
- Give demonstrations

Don't Ignore Any Mentions

Social media helps people connect with each other. While it might seem unimportant, you must engage with everyone who reaches out to you. If you ignore people on social media, you are damaging your brand.

KLOOBY SNACK
Gimmicks are not for everyone. If you do not want to use gimmicks, it is better to leave them alone. Better no gimmick than a poorly executed one.

It is essential that you address every **positive** and **negative** mention that you come across. Positive mentions are easy to address. Simply thank them for taking the time to provide positive feedback; not everyone takes the time to do this.

When handling negative mentions, begin by addressing misinformation. You should also apologize if you are in the wrong.

Before we move on to our most critical 11th and final tip of this section, we want to remind you that Vipul and I have real life experience with everything we've overviewed for you here … lots of wins and lots of failures and setbacks we've learned from. We really look forward to discussing strategic social media with you on our weekly tip reading in 2022!

T I P #11

PROTECT THE BRAND

 Your brand will face a crisis, no matter how prepared or well organized you are. When a crisis comes, you need to know how to handle the situation. Keep your head in a crisis and respond carefully. Acting precipitously will only damage your reputation and your brand. By addressing the problem head on, you will be able to mitigate the damage to your brand.

Caught in a Bad Spot?

There may come a time when you find yourself in a bad spot. For example, you could upload mistaken information in your area of expertise. You could also act against your own advice. Regardless of what you do to damage your reputation, never avoid facing your mistakes. You must take control of the situation and the message using specific steps:

- Act quickly and apologize
- Explain your error in judgment
- Learn from your mistakes

It is essential that you do not allow your mistakes to define you. Once you address the problem, you need to move on and continue expanding your brand.

Never Burn a Bridge

In difficult situations, you may be tempted to burn bridges, but you should

NEVER burn a bridge. Burning bridges is breaking ties with difficult people, be they at work or in your social network. When you burn a bridge, you walk away from someone with no hope of salvaging the relationship. Burning bridges at work can negatively affect your employment record. Burning bridges within your social group can do more than cost friends; it can create enemies.

Burning Bridge Alternatives:

- Wait to communicate until your anger has passed.
- Thank the person for his or her feedback.
- Consider your fault in the situation.
- Take space in the relationship without breaking ties.

Information

Problems in personal branding often stem from problems in communication. Miscommunication and misinformation happen regularly, and they can destroy your personal brand. It is essential that you address communication errors immediately and squelch rumors before they spread. Once a negative rumor spreads, like wildfire, it is difficult to stop the gossip train. This is why you need to monitor your online presence carefully.

Examples of misinformation:

- Business rumors
- Misquotations
- False claims
- Incorrect statistics

The best way to handle this situation is with the truth. Address the source of the misinformation directly and be sure to spread the truth throughout all of your public platforms.

Monitor and Respond

You must carefully monitor every crisis situation because time is of the essence. Gather all information about your brand as it appears online.

Google Alerts and other tools are useful for this task. You need to be aware of the situation in order to respond appropriately.

When you find errors being reported, respond immediately. Your response will depend on the message that you found. For example, you might need to clarify information to someone who posted about your brand. You could also need to confront someone with truth when everything said is false. Remember, though, it is important that you do not attack people in your responses. Your goal is to present the truth, not go on a personal crusade.

BUSINESS ACUMEN

T I P #1

BE THE BLIMP!

Imagine having the perspective of the quarterback in American football. You're trying to see downfield 80 yards to the end zone, while there are 21 other people on the field … and more if you count the referees … and this is to say nothing of the people and cameras and signage in the peripheral vision out of bounds, but still on the field level in plain sight. Did I mention that all 21 of the other players are bigger than you and 11 of them are trying to get you? When it comes to calling and executing a play with all that going on, it is difficult to see everything you'd ideally want to see and difficult to do what you want to do! You "want" to grow (advance down the field), but your job is also to survive (not lose yardage, turn the ball over or get hurt)!

Now, imagine having the perspective being inside of the Goodyear Blimp (they did not pay me to use them in this analogy, by the way), the legendary provider of aerial coverage for the country's most famous sporting events since before I was born! From up there, you can see both end zones without moving your head at all … you can see the sidelines, the crowd, even the parking lot and some of the traffic surrounding the stadium. When it comes to calling a play, you can see exactly what you want to see (how the defense is set up and how much space there is to operate, etc.) AND you are in no danger of turning the ball over or getting tackled/hurt. Thus, doing exactly what you want to do requires communicating what you see down to the field, where it can be totally understood by the players to execute.

Business is the same when it comes to the difference between the "transactional" duties of people working "in" the business and the "transformational" duties of the entrepreneur/owner who must work "on" the business. The quarterback is IN the game, looking/behaving within the game. The Goodyear Blimp is above the game, looking both on and around the game, and ultimately, promoting and growing the game! Be the Blimp!

Tip #1 in the Business Acumen section, Be The Blimp, isn't just to see the big picture. We think that's rather obvious, especially for entrepreneurs. What is less obvious and what we really want you to know about Tip #1 is that it is that you must see the big picture the way the Blimp sees its job: to provide aerial coverage!

Knowing what to look for when "seeing the big picture" can help you recognize things you may have missed and also help organize your "vision" in ways that empower the communication to "the players." Here's a short list of things to recognize and communicate "down to the field" when seeing your big picture:

- Market trends—including the impact of technology, regulation, politics, cultural factors, weather, international events or shifts in local demographics.
- Customer needs—it would be transactional to wait for a complaint before finding out what customers need. Get ahead of this with pro-active market research, such as surveys, interviews, focus groups, beta-runs, etc.
- Study competitors—sports teams like to say, "If we play to our capabilities, we will beat anyone!" We aren't sure that can ever be true in business. We believe it is critical to study the strengths, weaknesses, opportunities, and threats among the competition so you can make plans to differentiate and compete more effectively!
- Consult employees—we recommend getting out of the Blimp from time to time to get info from the people that you will continue providing aerial coverage for. The Blimp needs to be receptive to input from the fans. Employees have information that can inform the

owner/entrepreneur what to be looking for when looking for growth opportunity.

- What's possible—From a skills and abilities perspective, knowing what people are capable of doing may lead to growth opportunities. For example, the rapid adoption of "Zoom" technology (they aren't paying us, either) the COVID outbreak has shown what is possible for remote work and has represented growth opportunities through remote working that weren't visible before. Owners/entrepreneurs with the business acumen to "Be the Blimp" have most likely done a better job "providing aerial coverage" to their employees.

> Vipul and I LOVE helping clients see and communicate their big pictures!

TIP #2

KNOWING (YOUR) KPI'S

A simple definition of the word "statistics" is: numerical data. That's it. Information that is represented in numerical form. Even a date, like 7-4-1776, is a statistic. Statistics differ from non-numerical information in the very useful ways that they assist us in the understanding of size, magnitude, trends, probability, and fact, truth. or objectivity.

A Key Performance Indicator (KPI) is a question a business asks and answers in order to know if it is doing a good job or not. And be clear that a KPI is (must always be) a statistic expressed in numerical form that gives the business the information of size/magnitude, trends, probability and facts/truth/objective reality regarding its productivity and profits.

KLOOBY SNACK

Declaring your KPI's is a promise to measure something about your business!

It's not enough just to know what a KPI is … Tip #2 is also asking you to place priority, careful thought, and ultimately decisiveness into deciding what *your* KPI's are or will be. The goal line is 100 yards from the opposite goal line in American football. A first down to keep possession of the ball requires that ball travel 10 yards in 4 plays or less, and an average quarterback throws for about 250 yards per game. Do you see the numerical data that helps us know our KPI's?

But it's not that easy. Given the football example above, what is the better KPI if you own the team: How many yards per game your quarterback averages throwing? Or how many games per season your starting quarterback plays in?

Said another way, declaring your KPI's is a promise to measure something about your business! The entrepreneur/owner with true acumen will give consistent effort to knowing what must be measured. Here's a brief guide:

- What questions need to be answered? Are we growing? What areas of business are working, what areas need improvement, and how would we know? How do our employees know if they are doing well or not? How do we know if our employees are doing well? And many more!

- What's measured? This is determining more specifically what will be measured. How many new leads/prospects are we getting per month? How many new customers? How many repeat customers? How many referrals from customers? How many customer complaints? How many lost customers?

- What counts!? Just knowing how many missed days of work employees had in a given year isn't helpful without a standard of "attendance" for employees. Just knowing how many customers you have in a year isn't helpful unless you established a projection, budget, or criteria for what is below, average, or above average!

Finally, this tip began by establishing that KPI's must be a statistic… we end by saying that KPI's must not be "static," meaning, they must be set, but not set in stone. Entrepreneurs/owners must consistently review KPI's with the flexibility to make adjustments both to what is being measured and what counts as "good, bad or average" once measured.

> Vipul and I LOVE brainstorming KPI criteria with business owners, execs, and leaders of businesses and high-performance teams!

TIP #3

THE FIVE PILLARS OF BUSINESS MANAGEMENT

Tip #3 is somewhat a tease because it would be easy to create 52 brand new tips out of this single tip (not a bad idea, by the way). For this edition of GAKn52, we simply want you to know/prioritize the 5 pillars of management!

In no particular order, they are Risk, Talent, Change, Asset, and Organizational.

We'll start with Risk because we believe strongly that this is mostly likely among the first considerations: Is this business worth building/ having? What is the expense of starting, running, growing, keeping, or selling your business? Here is a quick six-step primer for Conducting Risk Assessment:

Risk Assessment Steps:

1. **Recognize objectives:** The scope of the assessment is based on specific objectives, created using SMART goals.

2. **Identify potential events:** Use prior and possible events to determine risks. Identify external factors, such as the economy, politics, technology, and the environment as well as internal data. The information identifies risks and opportunities.

3. **Identify risk tolerance:** Determine the variation from the objective that is acceptable with risks.

4. **Determine the probability and impact of risks:** Assign an impact and probability rating to risks based on data.

5. **Outline responses for risks:** Assign a response for each risk. These may be to accept, avoid, reduce, or share the risk.

6. **Determine the impact and possibility:** Evaluate the controls and response.

A second pillar of Business Management is Talent! The Human Resource department typically monitors talent management, but so many of the entrepreneurs/owners we have worked with do not have an HR staff, let alone a single employee dedicated solely to performing a company's HR duties. Still, smaller businesses, microbusinesses, or start-ups are subject to the same challenges, such as the high cost of turnover combined, poor engagement, competition for skilled labor, and need for succession planning, that a company with sophisticated HR has. That means it is most likely YOUR responsibility to manage talent. Here is a quick overview of the four stages to talent management.

1. **Assess:** Determine what your company needs done and the skills employees need in order to do it!

2. **Recruit:** Search for and recruit the right employees for the organization.

3. **Develop:** Train and develop employees to promote and stay long-term.

4. **Coordinate:** Align the goals of the employees with the goals of the company.

In the "Management Edition" of GAKn52, we'll have at least 10 Tips for Managing Talent and, of course, Vipul and I absolutely love coaching or consulting with clients in this area!

A third pillar of Business Management is Asset. Asset management is a plan that you implement to define your assets and how they are used. Mismanaged assets will affect your equity, credit, and reputation. Implementing asset management may be easier with the help of different software programs available. Of course, software is usually only as good as the data entered into it, so we really recommend coaching/advising for the back-n-forth sound boarding and critical thinking that software won't provide.

As we discussed above, your talent is certainly one of your best assets, but there are others to manage and strategies for doing so effectively! For now, here's an overview of four critical steps in Asset Management:

Steps:

Involve the departments: Determine which departments have assets that need management and coordinate with them. The individual departments are responsible for their assets.

Create a list: Create a list of assets, along with the price paid, maintenance, devaluation, and disposal costs. Each department should create its own list.

Identify assets to manage: Choose the different assets that require management. They might be physical, intellectual, etc.

Develop a plan: Use a separate plan for each of the following: facilities management, maintenance plan, capital development.

A fourth pillar of Business Management is Organizational! Organizational management is unique to each company, depending on structure, but entrepreneurs/owners with acumen recognize that each singular element is linked to others and manages each toward "integrity" with the others.

One of the most impactful modules I have made in coaching entrepreneurs/owners is represented in the diagram on the next page. It has placeholders for 12 Accountabilities organized into or above 4 basic departments (from left to right: Marketing, Sales, Operations and Finance).

We want you to tune in to our weekly online Tip-Reading to go over the 12 actual accountabilities. For now, we want you to see the interrelationship and integration of the various roles by department. From a diagram like this, it is easier to create position descriptions, operations manuals, onboarding and training plans, performance management and improvement plans, and other things that help manage workflow and productivity optimization. It might be surprising how many businesses are operating without an organizational chart or position descriptions to guide the efforts of the business.

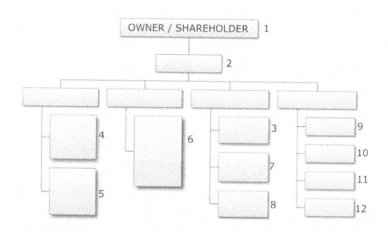

Finally, and perhaps the "scariest" pillar for you and your Talent, is Change Management! Change is inevitable in any organization, even a solo-preneurial operation! Unfortunately, human beings are not wired to accept change easily, so tensions may run high as people resist changes ... including you, the entrepreneur/owner. Regarding of the size of your business, smoothly implementing change will reduce lost productivity and improve workplace culture. There is so much more to discuss about Change Management than we'll cover here, but we will offer this overview of the process, assuming you have one or more employees.

3-Step Change Management Process:

1. **Prepare**:

   - **Define the change**: Identify the change, communicate with employees, and assess the needs, as well as potential resistance.
   - **Choose a team**: Find team members to lead the change.
   - **Sponsor**: Determine how leadership will actively sponsor the change.

2. **Manage**:

- **Develop plans**: Create a change management plan and communicate the details.
- **Act**: Implement the change management plan and continue to communicate the expectations.

3. **Reinforce**:

- **Analyze change**: Use surveys and feedback to determine success.
- **Manage resistance**: Understand the causes, look for gaps, and communicate the need for acceptance.
- **Correct or praise**: Praise individuals who implement change effectively and give corrective actions for resistance.

If you are a sole-preneur or a microbusiness owner, you may need to enlist a coach or your Peer Advisory group with your Change Management. You will most likely need some sort of outside perspective to help recognize your own need to change and the accountability to execute your own change!

Three things you can do with us to get more help in the five areas of management above:

- We've only scratched the surface! Buy and read *Get A Klu in 52, Management Edition* (due in Fall 2022) where we dive deeper with at least 10 more tips in each of the 5 areas.
- Join us on our Weekly Zoom, where we'll be reading one tip per week from this book. Ask us anything you want anytime or plan to be on specifically when we cover this topic (currently slated for the 14th week of the year).
- Schedule Two Complimentary Coaching Sessions with us or one of our trained coaches!

T I P #4

MISTAKE MANAGEMENT

Wow, that last tip was kinda long, especially for a tip that we were intentionally keeping as short as we could. By contrast, this tip is short and sweet. We assume you've heard it before, perhaps even 100 million times.

But can we say it in a fresh or sticky way? Can we say it in a way that cannot be ignored the way you've probably ignored it 100 million times? Okay, here it is as you have always heard it: Commit to continual learning ... always strive to learn! Learning is earning! Heard it before, right?

Well, how about seeing "learning" as important as the previous tip, 5 Pillars of Business Management? The 6th pillar of Business Management, in our opinion, is Mistake Management! And Mistake Management is one example of Mindset Management.

> **KLOOBY SNACK**
>
> There is no such thing as a mistake, just learning wrapped in the discomfort of growing pains.

Don't let the packaging fool you! On its surface (in our minds), a mistake is a bad thing because errors lead to a loss of time, money, opportunity, respect, trust, etc. Like an error in baseball, we are taught they are bad, costly. and to be avoided at all costs! Imagine a parent that is so afraid of their young toddler making a "mistake" that they are constantly screaming, "No, Don't, Stop, WAIT" hundreds of times per day. Imagine what that does to your mindset when it comes to what we think of "mistakes."

What we like to teach is that there is no such thing as a mistake, just learning wrapped in the discomfort of growing pains. Said another way, the only mistake to be afraid of is the one you do NOT learn from!

The best commitment to lifelong learning doesn't stop at continuing education, self-guided research, or certifications and skills trainings. The "acumen" level of learning is a commitment to and plan for learning from mistakes ... starting with the willingness to make them in the first place!

KLOOBY SNACK

The only mistake to be afraid of is the one you do NOT learn from!

Back to learning, here are different ways that people learn ... understand how best YOU learn and seek to know how your Talent learns to best prepare everyone in the organization to make and learn from our successes AND especially our mistakes!

8 Ways People Learn

1. **Imitation:** We learn from observing and imitating others, such as instructors or respected mentors.

2. **Reception/Transmission:** Reception is the experience that requires you receive a transmitted message. It may be written or verbal, and it can include values, as well as academic understanding.

3. **Exercise:** Actions and practice create learning experiences. These can occur in any action that you practice such as writing, meditation, or computer programs.

4. **Exploration:** Searching for answers or discovering information requires individual initiative. This comes from websites, interviews, books, etc.

5. **Experiment:** Experimenting or assessing the success of a project shows different possible outcomes and influences problem solving.

6. **Creation:** The creative process is also a learning process. These can be individual or group projects. The process ranges from painting to developing a new survey.

7. **Reflection:** Analysis before, during, or after an action is a learning opportunity. This can be done on a personal level or with the help of friends and colleagues.

8. **Debate:** Interactions with others cause us to defend or modify our perspectives. These are potential learning experiences.

> In the weekly live zoom we will do for this tip, I will take everyone through an exercise I created called "Mistake ROI," where I teach how to see mistakes as investments with very predictable RETURNS on those investments ... as long as we are willing to learn from them!

T I P #5

CORE COMPETENCY QUESTIONS

Running a business is a complex enterprise. In order to look at the big picture in your business, you need to know the answers to some basic financial questions. It is not enough that your accountant knows this information. Business acumen requires you to be aware of these answers so you will be able to guide your company to success.

What Makes My Company Money?

The purpose of every business is to make a profit. You need to make money in order to survive, but in order to do this, you must identify what makes your company money. You need to examine your products and services to determine which are actually making money for the company. For example, a bakery makes croissants, cookies, and cakes. The croissants account for 80% of the sales, and the cakes make up 15% of the sales. Cookies make up 5%, and some days most of them are thrown out. Knowing what makes your company money will provide influence and help steer the future of the company.

What Were Sales Last Year?

Companies need to grow to stay competitive. You are able to identify growth only when you see an increase in sales over time. Knowing last year's sales is essential to understanding the current status of your company. For example, you should use last year's sales to calculate the rate of change.

Rate of change:

1. Subtract the difference between last year's sales from this year's sales. Last year's sales were $90,000, and this year is $100,000.

$$100,000 - \$90,000 = \$10,000 \text{ increase}$$

2. Divide increase or decrease by the previous year.

$$10,000 / 90,000 = .111$$

3. Multiply the rate by 100.

$$.111 \times 100 = 11\% \text{ increase}$$

What is Our Profit Margin?

Every business needs to make a profit. The profit margin indicates how well the company is running. A large, successful company typically has a 13% net profit margin. The higher the profit margin, the more efficient the business is run. There are two types of profit margins: gross profit margin and net profit margin. Both are found when the profit is divided by the total revenue. The difference between the two is that the net profit margin is profit after tax and operating costs.

Example:

Revenue = $150,000

Gross profit = $50,000/150,000 = 33% gross profit margin

Net profit = $10,000/150,000 = 10% net profit margin

What Were Our Costs?

A company's costs affect other financial aspects, such as profits. This is why it is so important to control costs. Many companies choose to increase profits by cutting costs. However, this can backfire when the costs you cut directly affect the customers' experience.

Basic Costs:

COGS: Cost of goods sold is also called direct cost. This includes costs associated with production, materials, labor, inventory, distribution, and other expenses. The individual COGS must stay below the sale price to make a profit.

Operating expenses: Overhead expenses are included in operating expenses, which is any expense necessary to keep the company running that is not COGS. Examples include support function salaries, rent, marketing, R&D, utilities, equipment, travel, etc.

Interest and other expenses: Interest on loans or investment losses are not part of running the business from day to day, but they affect the bottom line. Other expenses include lawsuits and selling an asset.

Taxes: Federal, state, and local taxes are unavoidable costs of doing business.

Vipul and I know we have a potential client in front of us when their answer to the questions above "seem" vague, contradictory, illogical, suspicious, sensational/inflated, or are just flat out missing. And we know we have a potentially great client in front of us when they are honest about their answers to these questions, whatever that truth may be. The person who is honest is the person who wants to grow and improve!

If you don't have answers to these questions, consider taking us up on our offer of 2 Complimentary Coaching Sessions!

T I P #6

FINANCIAL LITERACY: TRANSACTIONAL

 Financial literacy is SO important to your overall business acumen that it literally deserves two tips. First, we'll discuss "transactional" financial literacy, and Tip #7 will cover "transformational" financial literacy.

By transactional, we mean that the meaning and life of the activity is self-contained in the transaction itself … another way I like to see it is "compliance" accounting in the sense that every transaction of a business needs to be documented and presentable for scrutiny in case of audit or disputes. By contrast,

KLOOBY SNACK

All transformational decisions are transactional, but vice versa is not true!

transformational refers to activities whose value is contained in the contribution the current activity makes to growth, such as the strategy of offering a desired candidate a signing bonus to leave their current position to join your company … that is a transformational decision. All transformational decisions are transactional, but vice versa is not true!

Like all of the tips in this book, Tip #6 can be stretched into over 100 tips, a full certification course, or even state license. The entrepreneur/owner is usually not also the accountant in need of such details or licensure, but still must have a certain basic financial literacy to effectively direct and manage the oversight of business accounting functions.

Here's a very simple summary of the key components of what we call "transactional" finance:

Income Statement 101

The income statement allows you to see what money the company made. It is also called a profit and loss statement because it shows the profits or losses for a period, typically a quarter or year. An income statement shows information from the two previous reports, allowing you to determine growth. Each income statement is unique, but there are six measures that need to be included.

Parts of an income statement:

Revenue: Sales or gross revenue

Cost of goods sold: COGS or the cost of sales

Gross profit: Revenue – COGS

Operating expenses and income: Itemize each expense to calculate income

Net income: Net profit

EPS: Earnings per share is for public companies

Other expenses and income may also be included, if necessary.

Balance Sheet Basics

A balance sheet shows you where your company stands at a given time by showing assets, liability, and equity. Balance sheets are prepared the last day of the month, quarter, or year. The balance sheet allows you to determine the financial health of an organization. While balance sheets are created based on the needs of each company, there are specific topics that need to be addressed.

Items on a balance sheet:

Current assets: specifically liquid assets

Total assets: includes long-term assets, such as investments

Current liabilities: liabilities paid within a year

Total liabilities: includes liabilities to be paid past 12 months

Stockholders' equity: Stockholders' equity is used in public trading. If the company is private, equity is the difference between total liabilities and assets.

Cash Flow Statement: Just State It!

A cash flow statement is exactly what it sounds like. It provides information about the cash generated and how it was used. It is also called a sources and uses of cash statement. Cash flow statements are usually generated every quarter or year and contain the three most recent reports. You can use the information in the cash flow statement to define the net increase or decrease in cash equivalents.

Simple Equations:

Cash from operations +/- cash from investments +/- cash from financing = Net increase or decrease

Each cash flow statement is unique, but there are specific items that should be included on the report.

Items on a cash flow statement:

Net cash (used or provided by) operating activities

Net cash (used or provided by) investing activities

Net cash (used or provided by) financing expenses

You begin the cash flow statement with the net income from the income statement, and it ends with the cash equivalent, the beginning of the balance sheet.

Finally: Read, Read, and Read

Financial literacy requires continuing education. Do not become complacent in your learning. Read everything that you find concerning financial literacy. Once you find pertinent information, consider different ways to integrate it into your company's financial strategies.

Sources of information:

- Books
- Periodicals
- Trade publications
- Government publications
- Blogs/websites
- Databases
- 2 Complimentary Coaching Sessions with Jeff and Vipul! ☺

TIP #7

FINANCIAL LITERACY: TRANSFORMATIONAL

In Tip #6, we recommended developing a basic competence for Transactional Finance. As the entrepreneur/owner, we believe your acumen further develops when you demonstrate a literacy for transformational finance. Again, by that we mean the activities whose value resides more in the future value created for the growth of the business vs. the immediate value of a transactional activity.

Remember, in Tip #2, we advised to you "Be The Blimp" by seeing the big picture and also ensuring the most effective communication OF that big picture to your Talent! The following overview of Transformational Finance basics are the perfect lenses through which to see the big picture, as well as the perfect devices with which to communicate to your Talent.

Establish, Grow, Reinvest In, and Reinvest Your Assets!

Assets are anything of value that the company has that will create a profit or improve revenue. Many assets are listed on a balance sheet, such as a building or product. Some assets, however, are not listed on the balance sheet. Assets such as customers and employees are not listed, but they are the most valuable assets that companies have.

A company's strength is determined by its assets, especially its liquidity. A liquid asset is cash or is easily converted to cash, making it more stable in times of emergency. However, businesses are not supposed to hoard cash; they are meant to invest in other assets and utilize them to increase the return in productivity. For example, you may purchase a machine that increases production. The key is balancing liquid assets with the assets you utilize.

Financial Ratios

Financial ratios are formulas that provide information about the company's status. The information used to find financial ratios is typically taken from the financial statement. Ratios are used to find a variety of information, including trends, liquidity, profitability, assets, and financial leverage. We have already examined some ratios in the previous module. The following are some more basic ratios you will need to navigate your financials.

Ratio Formulas:

ROA (Return on Assets) = Net income/Total assets x 100

Inventory Turnover = Cost of Goods Sold/ Inventories

Revenue Sales Growth = This year's revenue/ last year's revenue -1 x 100

Earnings Per Share Growth = This year's EPAs/Last year's EPAs -1 x 100

Liabilities

Liabilities are monies that you owe or a debt. Mortgages or credit balances are liabilities. Liabilities are a measure of financial health. Too many liabilities are an indication that the company is in trouble, particularly if the liabilities exceed the assets. Liabilities may be short term or long term. Short-term liabilities are considered mature within a year, and they typically have lower interest rates. Long-term liabilities last longer than a year. They are a greater risk and have higher interest rates.

Equity

Both assets and liabilities are used to determine equity. Your equity, in turn, will determine what type of business risk you are. Lending institutions and investors examine your equity carefully. Good equity is associated with being a low-risk investment, and it makes you a low-risk borrower.

Equity Equation:

Assets – liabilities = Equity

Essentially, equity is what you have left after paying off all of the debts that you owe.

Issuing stocks to shareholders can create equity. For stockholders, equity is what they would have after liquidation. A higher equity ratio indicates that they will earn more money.

Equity Ratio = Shareholder equity/Assets x 100

Understanding equity and what it influences is necessary to improve your business acumen.

Personally, I got lucky and married an accounting and finance wizard, but not all entrepreneurs/owners are so lucky. As a communication and "soft skills" guy, you can imagine how uninterested I am in spreadsheets and number crunching. Truth is, I am not. But that does not relieve me of the responsibility of knowing enough to guide the work that my wife (as CFO in my business) and CPA (tax preparer for my business) does for my business. I have to be smart enough to guide and work with them effectively.

Vipul LOVES conversations about numbers, honestly, a lot more than I do. But I will be happy to join you for 2 Complimentary sessions with Vipul if you want help with your financial literacy ... transactional or transformational. We are here for you!

T I P #8

CRITICALLY THINK YOUR WAY
TO BETTER DECISIONS

 In business, you are constantly bombarded with information. You rely on this information to make important decisions. Business acumen requires that you do more than absorb information. You need to think critically about information and make your decisions accordingly.

Ask the Right Questions

Critical thinking requires you to ask questions continually. You should question people, information, plans, etc. The key to critical thinking is asking the right questions. The questions should:

- Identify assumptions: Is it verified?
- Explore perspectives: What is another point of view?
- Examine evidence: Why did this occur?
- Attempt to understand: What do you mean?
- Consider different implications: Is this important?

For example, a critical thinking question about statistics would be, *"Is this source credible?"* By asking the right questions, you will weed out useless or harmful information and utilize the information that will help you in your endeavors.

Organize Data

Critical thinking and decision making requires you to analyze different data sets. Organizing your data will make it easier for you to analyze. There are programs that will help you get organized. Data may be grouped together for specific reasons, or they may follow certain patterns. For example, you would want to group financial statements together when organizing data. Once you organize your data, you will see trends emerge as you draw conclusions. For example, market trends will become apparent once you organize your research on external business factors. The trends that you see in the data will help guide and shape your business.

Evaluate the Information

You must always evaluate information and conclusions before making any decisions. You should differentiate between a fact and an opinion by using the right questions. You also need to identify information and conclusions for any signs of bias. For example, does a conclusion you are reading consider all of the information available? Even when information is factually based, it might not be relevant to the argument, which indicates possible bias. For example, the fact that it was cold one night does not provide information about the lunar cycle. You need to identify facts that are relevant, substantial, and applicable before you draw your own conclusion from the information presented.

Make the Decision

Critical thinking is useful in the decision-making process. You already know how to ask questions and evaluate information. Once you have done both, you have a few more considerations before you make the decision. Once you have evaluated everything, make the decision and act on it. You can feel secure knowing that you based your decision on accurate and relevant information.

The effects of your decision: How will the decision affect you, your business, and others? Is the effect long term or short term?

Options: Do you have more than one option?

Your feelings: Are you comfortable with the decision?

In our weekly LIVE Zoom for this tip, remind us to also present the 5 Barriers to Critical Thinking and reveal the 5 automatic behaviors (that we are ALL guilty of) that prevent us from asking questions, listening, being objective and ... dare I say, loving! Be sure you join us LIVE on our weekly zoom session for more on critical thinking your way to better business decisions!

T I P #9

THREE LEVERS THAT POWER BUSINESS

 Imagine a lever, like an old-fashioned light switch ... two positions, up or down. In the up position, the lever opens a passageway for electricity to get to the light bulb, and in the down position that energy is cut off.

There are three critical levers in every business and knowing what they are with a plan to keep them in or constantly turn them to the "on" position is a crucial step toward business acumen.

Using all P-words, the three levers are People, Processes, and Potential. We'll explain.

Investing in People

People are a key financial lever in any business; people are your greatest asset. The people associated with your business are your customers and your employees. If you do not invest in your people, you are making a disastrous mistake.

Employees: Many companies cut back on expenses related to employees to save money. However, this can backfire and cost you qualified people. Consider investing in employees in the following ways:

- Training
- Bonus
- Fair salary
- Relationships

- Opportunity for advancement

Customers: Your job is to anticipate customer needs and wants. You invest in your customers when you offer them what they need. Consider the following customer investments:

- Create new products
- Develop a customer experience
- Improve relationships

Process Improvement

Process improvement is used to analyze business processes. It is also used to introduce a new process or changes to existing ones. Benefiting from process improvement requires you to follow some basic steps:

Steps to Improvement:

Identify: Identify processes to change and prioritize the order of the change process.

Establish measures: Determine objectives and measures used to determine the performance.

Determine and validate: Determine if there are obstacles and the exact path necessary to reach objectives.

Support: Get buy in from leadership.

Data: Collect and analyze data from surveys, metrics, etc.

Options: Provide different change options.

Revise: Revise the project based on the options chosen.

Implement: Use change management strategies to implement a plan.

Approval: Gain acceptance from stakeholders.

Evaluate: Evaluate the success of the process.

Potential and Its Milestones: Goals!

Part of looking at the big picture of business is goal alignment. Goal alignment is aligning the goals of all managers and employees with the goals of the business. The goals of the business are the MILESTONES toward its mission and ultimately potential!

Aligning individual goals is done at the team level. For example, a team goal to increase production 10% over the next month will affect the individual goals. Team goals are based on the information from cascading goals.

Cascading goals start with the Vision and Mission from the top of the company and change as they cascade down to the different employee levels. Once you have team goals, you can identify your individual goals.

Remember, they must be based on company goals, and remember that we teach SMAART goal setting where goals are: Specific, Measurable, Achievable, Ambitious, Rewarded, and Timely.

Vipul and I love to work with entrepreneurs/owners in developing their vision and mission statements and then, from those, helping the rest of the organization with annual objectives and quarterly SMAART goals at the team and individual levels.

In our weekly zoom session for this tip, or privately in your own 2 complimentary coaching sessions with Vipul and/or myself, ask us to explain how we distinguish Vision from Mission from Objectives from Goals. For now, understand that the entrepreneur/owner with business acumen uses these sub-sets of Potential to help guide the business more effectively toward it!

T I P #10

COMMUNICATION ACUMEN

IS BUSINESS ACUMEN

Another thing you have heard 100 million times is "communication is key" or "communication is the solution to every problem" or any cliché (which is a code word for "catchy way of saying the truth" since a cliché is usually truth-based) about the importance of communication in business and relationships, etc.

Nobody tells you, though, HOW to get better at communication! Who can tell you the difference between good and bad communication, between effective communication and miscommunication, between informative communication and persuasive communication?

Most people believe themselves to be great communicators, but it is everyone else who sucks. There are fewer people who actually believe they need to get better at communicating, but so many of those people never actually commit to take action to learn how to improve communication.

KLOOBY SNACK

Regardless how much we know, how much experience we have, or how right we are, none of it matters unless we communicate effectively.

Then there are the very rare people, like Vipul, who makes commitments and investments in himself to be better in all of his businesses! Vipul hired me to be his coach back in 2015 because, among other things, he wanted to be a better communicator! Vipul realized, regardless of how much he knew, how much experience he had, or how RIGHT he was, that none of it mattered unless he could communicate effectively.

I have a master's in communication and retired in 2017 from a twenty-year career as an Adjunct Professor of Communication. Now I teach communication privately in my coaching, soft skills trainings, retreats/masterminds, and online e-courses. I love helping people improve their communication skills and REALLY LOVE helping organizations solve communication-related problems, mostly because MOST business problems are communication problems.

Similarly, Communication Acumen is something we believe to be synonymous with Business Acumen!

OWNERSHIP

T I P #1

PAY THE FEE OF FEASABILITY!

 Very simply put, is the business worth owning? Whether you start it from scratch, buy it, or inherit it, you must first ask yourself, "Is this business worth owning?"

The challenge is in "knowing" that a business is worth owning when we "believe" it is worth owning without making the effort to find out for sure. That is the "pay" we refer to when playing with the word "feasibility"... the "fee" sound allows us to give you this tip: PAY the FEE of Feasibility!

Feasibility describes how simple it is to accomplish something. So, question #1 is: what do you want your business to accomplish? Why does the business exist? What is the purpose of the business? Then we can start assessing how easy or difficult it will be to accomplish that purpose. People get into trouble when their answers to these initial questions are too auto biographical. Examples:

- I have always wanted to have my own business.
- I am too over-qualified for any decent jobs out there.
- I am really passionate about (insert hobby here _____).
- I just feel like it's time to do something else.
- People have always told me I am good at (insert talent/ability here _____).
- I just don't want to work for another boss I don't respect.
- I really want to help people.

Now this last example, "I really want to help people," is only a bad answer to the initial questions IF that is all there is to it … if it's just about you wanting to help.

However, IF you can go on to describe the *exact* problem that *specific* people are having AND IF you can continue with *how your product or service helps solve* that specific problem for those specific people, you are on your way to understanding if your business if feasible or not. THEN you are ready to ask the next set of questions that you are NOT ready for if the only reason to own a business is looming in the samples above! ☺

Examples of the next sets of questions you'll need to ask/answer in order to determine if your business idea is feasible, include:

- Do you have the necessary funding?
- Is there a market for your product, and how will you inform the market about your solution?
- What is the outlook for the market, and who is your competition?
- Can you price competitively or promote other competitive advantages?
- Is anything about your business "protectable" from a patent perspective?
- How would you operate?
- Would you have a sufficient customer base for long-term success?

Our intent is not to oversimplify with the sample questions above, but instead to be clear that the first "hard work" you must put into your business is "paying the fee of feasibility" to get to a "knowing" (vs. just "believing") that your business is worth owning!

Vipul and I LOVE to discuss business viability! Consider scheduling two complimentary sessions with us to discuss the viability your business ideas!

T I P #2
C THE MARKET!

Our first tip in the Ownership section was about knowing the feasibility of your business. A huge part of knowing feasibility is knowing the market. "The market" refers to "where" that business will take place. And by "where," it is important to go beyond just location. It is critical, in this context, to imagine everything ABOUT the "where" that is critical to achieving your purpose for owning the business.

Conveniently, there are 4 C-words that effectively categorize the major things you will want to know about The Market. Knowing the market is critical in deciding how to inform the market about your business. Informing the market will be discussed in Tip #7 in this section: B the Market.

Meanwhile, this tip wants you to C the Market! Here are the four critical aspects of your marketplace we strongly recommend knowing and sample questions we use in our coaching sessions with clients that explain how important each of the C's are!

- **Customers:** Who is your ideal customer? What are the demographics and psychographics of your customer? Can you tell your customer's story? Do you know the self-talk your customer has when dealing with the problem you want to help them solve? How do you plan to continually gather information about and from your customers?
- **Conditions/Climate:** What is happening socially, politically, economically, culturally, spiritually, structurally, geographically, environmentally, or otherwise in your marketplace? How do the conditions of the market influence your customers and their decision

making? What aspects of market conditions require planning and adaptability in your business? Are there predictable occurrences or observable trends in marketplace conditions that help or hinder your ability to serve our customers/clients?

- **Competition:** Who are you competing with? Who else sells to your customers, and who else sells the same thing(s) you are selling to them? Who else is your customer choosing from, and what advantages does your competition have that you don't have? Can you list your top competitors and learn/be honest about why a customer would choose them, instead of you?

- **Competitive Advantages:** Can you really compete? If so, how? Do you compete on price, service, quality, selection, rewards programs, convenience, or any other brand promise? Do you know what you have or do BETTER than the competition that has/does the same thing? Do you know what you have or do that the competition simply does NOT have or do? Do you know how to communicate your competitive advantages to your customers in the marketplace, given the current/predictable conditions?

Vipul and I will tell you that there are many more questions to ask and answer than just those we sampled above. And we LOVE helping clients go deeper in their understanding of their market because we know that will help them put better messages OUT into that marketplace!

B the Market ("branding" the market) is Tip #7 in this section ... that gives you five weeks to research your C's! We hope to see you online with us for our weekly rip reading when we cover the "info in" and "info out" of knowing/informing you market!

T I P #3

PURPOSES OF PLANNING

Proper planning prevents piss poor performance ... a friend of mine once told me the lesson that his father or grandfather taught him. Failure to plan is planning to fail ... another way of describing the value of planning that you may have heard before.

Vipul and I know that you probably already know or have heard (above or otherwise) how important it is to have a plan ... know the plan ... stick to the plan ... have a backup plan ... know when to abort the plan, etc.

Yet, we also know that most entrepreneurs/owners do NOT have a business Plan. It is very much like goal setting in that most people will tell you that they know the importance of having/setting goals, but research has proven that less than three percent of our population actually sets or writes down their goals.

Vipul and I also know the myriad of reasons entrepreneurs/owners think they do not need a plan "yet," or "right now," or "when things aren't as crazy," etc.

Tip #3 is a summary of what we feel are the major purposes of having a business plan. If after reading this tip, you still wish to proceed without a plan, so be it. Otherwise, we love providing supporting coaching, sound boarding, role playing, and additional resources to help clients with business planning. First, why plan?

- **FEASABILITY:** Tip #1 got you started on the road to discovering feasibility with a focus on the mindset of being willing to do the work of knowing ... we offered some sample questions of feasibility in that tip; whereas, here, we suggest that the effort to draft a business plan will force you to answer ALL questions of feasibility! You will know if your business is worth having/running if you even draft a business plan.

- **MONEY:** If your business needs a source of outside funding, you will need a plan that shows: how much you need, what it will be used for, how that application will participate in profitable revenue, and over how much time and in what form the money will be paid back. Let us be clear that EVEN IF you are the ONLY one funding your business, you should have the exact same questions answered "by" the business "for" yourself.

- **CULTURE:** A plan allows the entrepreneur/owner to declare their "why." In the form of a vision, mission, or values statement, or the updating and promoting of objectives in annual versions of the plan, the company develops a guideline for the behavior and decisions of its people. The employee that cannot get an immediate answer to a "what should I do" question can always lean on the vision, mission, objectives, and values codified in the company's plan for guidance. A plan is an objective way for a company to establish "how we do things," "what we stand for," "what we believe in," and "the impact we wish to make." These things can be communicated in team meetings, one-on-one's, at the water cooler, or on the walls of the building in motivational quote art … all of which is more effective when codified first and foremost by the company's business plan!

- **GROWTH/SUCCESSION PLANNING:** There are two main things we feel your business is responsible for "growing," and that is Revenue and People! A smart business will anticipate and plan for both. One of my favorite coaching questions to ask business owners is: If your business tripled tomorrow, do you have everything in place that you would need to handle that volume effectively (same quality, customer satisfaction, etc.)? It goes back to the simple saying that if you are not growing, you are dying. So what plans does the business have to grow, to expand, to reinvest in its success? And how do the people grow within the business? Is there a path for raises, bonuses, benefits, promotions, and ultimately retirement in your business? How will your business attract and keep great people? When the business succeeds in the market, what is the plan to replicate and expand that success? When people succeed inside the business, what is the plan to reward and encourage that productivity?

- **EXIT STRATEGY:** And what about your personal succession plan? Many entrepreneurs/owners do everything in the business when starting out and get buried/trapped working "in" the business and never work "on" the business in a way that gets them OUT of the business! So what IS the "exit strategy?" Is there one? Will the business die with you, or do you have a plan to sell it? Pass it on (to someone who actually wants it!) through inheritance? Donate the business to a non-profit? What does the business need to do, achieve, have, look like in order for you to exit from it? Do you have a plan you are working toward to remove yourself from the business? Or again, will the business become your life and ultimately die with you?

Vipul and I recommend reading *The E-Myth Revisited* by Michael Gerber, a wonderful parable about the best pie baker in town who was convinced by the community to open her own pie shop. The struggles she has are a wonderful way to reveal the problems that most have and the reasons most small business fail in their first 1-5 years—problems that can be eliminated or easily solved with proper planning!

T I P #4

OPEN THE BUSINESS

 For the entrepreneur/owner, the business starts with the idea and imagination ... the business exists in your mind well before the business actually exists in a form visible to others! In Tips 1, 2, and 3 of this section, you have: decided that your business idea is feasible, studied your market, and drafted your business plan. Now, the business has gone from your head to perhaps your computer or file cabinets as you accumulate research and refine your plan.

Tip #4 says it is now time to actually get the business OUT of your head, computer, or desk drawers and into the actual marketplace! You are ready to actually start the business now! Here is a very simple overview of the five basics steps that allow you to start conducting business!

Decide on a Name

Choosing a name is harder than it seems. You want the name to stand out and reflect your image. Names that are similar to competitors will not help you stand out, and they could result in lawsuits. If you are having difficulty coming up with a name, consider hiring a naming firm for assistance.

Tips to naming:

- Consider wordplay, but avoid cheesy puns
- Stick to basics; you shouldn't have to explain the name
- Consider your name as a domain; it should be short and easy to recall.

Legal Structure of the Business

Before taking any action, you must determine the legal structure of the business. There are legal structures for any type of company that you want, and each has its benefits and drawbacks. Choosing the correct structure will require you to understand what you expect from your company.

Types of businesses:

- **Sole proprietorship** – The simplest business to create also has the greatest financial risk because it includes limitless personal liability.
- **General partnership** – A business run by two or more individuals where all partners are responsible for the actions of one, if made in the name of the business.
- **Limited partnership** – The power to make decisions is limited to specific individuals and is outlined in the business plan.
- **C Corporation** – Corporations are taxed separately from the owners. They are taxed on both corporate dividends and shareholder dividends.
- **S Corporation** – Profits are passed through the IRS tax election, allowing the profit to go through the personal tax return, which prevents double taxation.
- **LLC** – Limited liability corporations are similar to partnerships and sole proprietorships but taxed like S corporations.

Register the Business

Once you have a name and chosen a structure, you need to register your business and obtain the appropriate licenses, permits, and identification. This will all depend on your state and your business.

- **EIN:** Unless you are working alone, you will probably need an EIN or employer identification number from the IRS.
- **DBA:** A doing business as or DBA is typically filed at the county clerk's office when the company does not use the owner's name. Some states do not require this, so it is important to check.
- **Business licenses and permits:** Business licenses are issued on federal and state levels and vary with the business. Federal licensing is required

for alcohol, agriculture, transportation, etc. It is always important to check with federal, state, and local guidelines to ensure that you have all licenses and permits needed.

Choose the Location

 The location of your business needs to be chosen carefully. Begin by determining if you are limited by any zoning regulations, such as agriculture or industry. Next, you must weigh safety and cost. Choosing a safe location will help draw customers and employees because they will not feel fearful in your business.

Other Considerations:

- **Image**: Choose an area that reflects your image (edgy, artsy, upscale, etc.).
- **Competition**: Choose an area where you complement your neighbors, rather than increase competition.
- **Growth**: Consider the opportunity for growth in the near future. If that is your plan, you will need extra space.

Hire an Accountant

You should have a trusted accountant from the beginning. When finding an accountant, you want someone to do more than prepare taxes. You want someone who will advise your business. Keep a few things in mind when choosing candidates:

- Experience with your type of business
- Expertise in the industry
- Services offered
- Will you work directly with the accountant?

Do not hire anyone who does not offer the services that you need or you feel uncomfortable working with in a business relationship.

Vipul and I love consulting with entrepreneurs/owners prior to the "starting the business" phase because sometimes, it is NOT a business that needs to be built around your idea. Knowing that before Tip #3 could be super valuable.

If you have already started a business in the past, you already know the above … but perhaps you can remember how you learned it and if having a book like this back then would have been useful? At any rate, on to Tip 5!

T I P #5

GET FINANCING

When you join our weekly tip reading for "Get Financing," we will all be leaning on Vipul and his expertise in this area. Vipul has both gotten financing for his businesses, and he has provided financing/investments for other businesses. I am always entertained when learning from him in this area.

Personally, I financed my own business with bubble gum and paper clips. Seriously, I remember putting my coaches training tuition on a credit card in 2007, when limits were maxed during the beginning of the worst economy since the Depression. I remember putting every dollar I earned back into the business, never taking salary but "living" in the business to write off as many expenses as we could. I never acquired financing in any of the ways we are about to summarize for you in this tip. Be clear that among the two of us, Vipul is the man when it comes to financing. I can't wait to watch you learn from him in our weekly live online tip reading!

Meanwhile, here's a summary of "basics" when it comes to getting financing for your business:

Get Financing

Financing sounds like a frightening word, but it doesn't have to be. Any viable business startup needs to be financed, and these days there are many different options for financing. Talking to people who have already taken the journey you're about to embark on is a great way to start. The next step will be exploring all of your options. Let's discuss what is on the road ahead.

Contact Organizations for Guidance

The more informed you are, the better equipped you will be to make the right decisions on financing for your business. Via mentors and informational websites, there are many organizations dedicated to helping fledgling businesses. Contacting one or more of these organizations and discussing with people who understand your needs is a crucial step as it provides some great information.

The SCORE association is a nonprofit organization that is dedicated to helping businesses. They have retired and volunteer executives on staff to mentor entrepreneurs. They also provide workshops, seminars, and a wealth of information on their website. While some of their services may cost a little money, many of their services are free to use. Here are some websites and associations to go to for help:

- **The U.S. Small Business Administration** - *Offers tips on financing your business with government assistance-* sba.gov
- **Business USA** - *Offers lots of information and resources for a business-*business.usa.gov
- **SCORE** -*Offers tons of information, mentoring, and resources-* score.org
- **Entrepreneur** - *Offers advice, information, and some services. They also have a magazine publication-*entrepreneur.com

Are there more sites and organizations out there to help you? Yes, there are!! These are just a few, so go out there, and get informed!

Decide the Type of Financing

Now that you have resources to get information about your financing, it's time to decide what type of financing you are looking for. It is imperative that you take the time to consider your options carefully. Choosing the wrong type of financing could sink your company before it even gets a chance to float. Here are a few of the different types of financing options:

- **Self-financing:** Self-financing means that you provide the funds needed to start the business. According to *Entrepreneur* magazine, it is the number one source of start-up financing for small businesses. You can save money, or use preexisting savings, borrow against your 401k, use the funds in your IRA, borrow against your life insurance, or take out a home equity loan.

- **Grants:** There are many different types of grants available. Some grants are state and regional grants; some are based on minority, veteran status, and the type of business you are trying to start. While there's lots of competition for grants, they are a great option—you don't have to pay them back!

- **Financing from friends or family members:** Friends or family members who have extra money and want to help see your business vision come to life are a great resource for financing. The downside to using financing from family and friends is you have to be very clear about when their investment can be returned to them.

- **Financing from bank loans:** Bank loans are a great option for financing. Bank loans are based on your credit, a solid business plan, experience, assets, and a personal guarantee that the loan will be paid back. If you are taking the bank loan route, be sure to contact different banks and get the best interest rate.

- **Financing from investors:** The three most common types of investors are private equity, venture capital, and angel investing. Private equity investors are usually made by individuals or privately owned companies. Venture capital investors are also from private equity, but they tend to be more hands on; they bring managerial or technical knowledge to help grow the business. Last, angel investing is a person who invests in businesses that do not get the attention of venture capitalists. These investors usually gain stock or equity in the company.

Shop Around

You wouldn't go to a car lot and buy the first car you see, would you? Not likely. You want to shop around and see what is available. Just like in any major purchase or financial commitment, you want to explore your options. Starting a business is a major life and financial event. Rushing into the first financing option you have is not the best course of action. Talk to as many business owners as you can and see where they got their financing. Go to multiple banks, if you are looking for a loan, and try to get the best rates. Contact your government agencies and explore what grants you are qualified for. Shop around for the best equipment and building prices. It won't cost you money to shop around, but it might cost you if you don't! We have all done it, bought something (like a pair of shoes) and found out that another store had the same thing for a lower price! Do yourself a favor and don't make that mistake with such a large financial commitment. Look around and make sure the grass isn't greener somewhere else!

What to Do Once Approved

Once you have finally gotten your start up funded, it's time for the hard work to begin. This is the time when you need to procure a place of business and the materials you need. This could range from buying paper clips to buying huge production machines. You will need to stay in constant contact with your accountant to make sure you are on budget. To stay within budget, it is best if you have a clear list of what is needed. You will want to check with different companies to see if they have your materials at lower prices. If you have received financing from investors, you will want to keep them in the loop about the progress. Also, check with your local government to acquire any needed permits or licenses.

T I P #6

FACING FINANCING FACTS

Again, and very honestly, money and finances are not my favorite part of being an entrepreneur/owner or coaching them. I am really a communication nerd, and while numbers speak a certain language, they don't attract me. Thank God my wife loves it and has handled it for me very well over the years. I am equally grateful to work so closely with Vipul and his expertise in matters of finance.

That might be why we use the term "facing" in this tip's title ... we believe I am not alone when it comes to not enjoying the numbers part of business. We also know that most entrepreneurs/owners do not know their numbers as effectively as they could, if at all. So, let's face it! In this tip, we suggest you'll need to know the critical facts when it comes to the numbers of running your business: procurement, budgets, sales, expenses, and cash flow!

Run the Business

Running the business can easily be seen as the "fun part." This is where you take all of the tools acquired to prepare you for operating a successful business and put them into practice. Before you can sell the products/services your company offers, you must source the materials. Once you do and the cash starts coming in, responsible money management and budgeting will prove to be your company's best friends.

Procurement

If your business consists of selling products and even for some services, you must source suppliers to provide the items to you and create a Master Agreement with them. Having a master agreement that clearly outlines the terms and prices will allow the transactions between you and the sellers to run more smoothly.

How do you find suppliers?

There is no hard rule on how your company should locate suppliers, but here are some steps that can help along the way.

- Have all interested suppliers complete a questionnaire. Make sure the questionnaire is comprehensive, asking all of the questions necessary for you to select the right supplier for your company.
- From all interested applicants, select a small group of the most qualified candidates. Send a request for proposal (RFP) to these candidates. In the RFP, discuss the products and/or services you require, as well as other pertinent details (e.g. timeline).
- Those who are still interested will submit a proposal to supply for your company.
- Select the supplier that best meets your needs.

Sell! Sell! Sell!

Most people think, "Selling a product (or service), that's easy!" While this may come naturally for some, effectively selling is not so easy for others. It is important to create a method for selling, rather than haphazardly doing so. This is a business, and one of your main goals is to make money. In order to make money on a consistent basis, carefully consider these steps:

- When you make initial contact with your prospective customer, greet him/her. You'd be amazed at how much this gets overlooked. Keep in mind, a little acknowledgment goes a long way!

- Get to know what the prospective customer needs. How can you intelligently discuss the benefits of your products/services if you don't know how they can meet the customer's needs?
- Restate the customer's needs. It is important to confirm you have properly understood what the customer wants. This will save a lot of time and headache on the back end.
- Develop a plan of action to meet the customer's desires.
- Simply ask for the sale.
- Close the deal.
- Follow up with the customer. Selling is not just about the sale; it is also about relationship-building. A repeat customer is the best customer to have.

How to Manage Cash Flow

 It is not necessary to be an accountant in order to manage your cash flow, but you must understand basic accounting principles. First, you need to know what cash flow is. Cash flow is the phrase used to describe the funds that come in and go out of a business. If you have positive cash flow, that means you have more money coming in than going out. That means, negative cash flow is … you guessed it … more money going out than coming in.

A company that has positive cash flow is not something that happens on its own; the business has to implement strategies that promote such.

What are some ways to improve cash flow?

- Increase your sales
- Don't extend as much credit to customers
- Give your customers pricing discounts

Budgeting

Budgeting should be a major component of every business, large or small. It serves two purposes: 1) It allows the company to estimate that which is spent on expenditures. 2) Companies can use the figures at the end of a specified period to determine if the company has stayed on budget and how this has affected its bottom line.

Before you can create a budget, you must know what you are working with. First, determine what you want to measure. Do you want to keep track of what you spend on supplies, personnel, and marketing? Then you need to gather all of the receipts, documents, and information that pertains to those items. You need an idea of the reasonable costs of those expenditures, as well as figure ways to decrease the amount of money you have spent on them in the past. This will help you make better predictions of how to set your budget.

Deciding on the method of budgeting to use depends on your business needs, as well as your personal preferences.

Some options are:

- **Zero-Based Budgeting**: This type of budgeting starts with a "zero baseline." All expenses must be justified each period.

- **Top-Down Budgeting**: Cost projections start at the highest level of the company (i.e., executives), then come down.

- **Bottom-Up Budgeting**: Cost projections start at the departmental level with employees, then go up.

Many of you might skip this tip if your business already has these systems and measures in place. Others might be overwhelmed at how much you have been ignoring and simply do not know about your own business. Others might be somewhere in between.

Vipul and I believe we can help you install or refine your ability to run your business "by the numbers." Consider engaging us for two complimentary sessions!

T I P #7

B THE MARKET!

Tip #2 in this section was: "C the Market" and described four C-words that represent the major things about the market that we want to know. It is about market "research," bringing information about the market IN to the company to create better decisions.

As promised, Tip #7 is about info OUT! When we say, "B the Market," we are asking you to BRAND the market! A lot of people use the word brand when they are talking about a company name or logo or a company's success story or stock price. In our opinion, none of those things are "the brand."

We believe a brand, any brand, is simply a promise to the marketplace. Branding is the process of getting the promise OUT to the marketplace. Below, you will see a rather generic summary of traditional ways to get "your message out to the marketplace" to generate leads, prospects, and ultimately customers.

The work you did in Tip #2 to know your market should put you in a position to create messages that are more compelling in the marketplace you are advertising to. Before you pick the channels/places for your messaging, we encourage you to create better messaging!

A brand is the promise, and the process of branding is all the ways you let the marketplace know about your promise.

A promise is good if it gets someone out of pain or closer to pleasure. Pleasure and pain are the only motivators in life. What pain can you promise to get your customers out of? What pleasure do you promise you can provide for your customers? And what is the biggest promise you can possibly make that you know you can back up?

Ultimately, the effectiveness of any brand is determined by if and how well a business delivers on its brand promise. A lot of companies have had great branding that generated a lot of customers only to have bad customer service or faulty products/services that failed to deliver on the promise. Giving refunds might be a worse feeling than never making sales in the first place!

> **KLOOBY SNACK**
>
> The effectiveness of any brand is determined by if and how well a business delivers on its brand promise.

To the greatest degree possible, all forms of outbound marketing (advertising, networking, social media, website, print/broadcast media) should include the brand promise and competitive advantages you identified in Tip #2. Tell the market what you can promise and WHY you can promise it!

Here's that generic summary of basic "ways" to market your business—remember at all times to do your best to "brand" the market with your promises and advantages!

- **Traditional Marketing:** The most common marketing environments are television, print, and radio advertising. TV commercials are excellent for getting information about your company and product out to a wide audience. In a commercial, you can demonstrate the product or service for the consumer in a controlled arena. The drawback to television advertisements is that they can be costly. If your service or product is able to be captured in a picture, then print ads may be what you need. A print ad can be in a newspaper, magazine, local publication, fliers, or billboards. The print ad has a wide variety of applications and prices. Last, radio commercials are great for businesses that provide services or have a product that can be described effectively in a short amount of time. The drawback to radio ads is that if you are selling something that has strong ties to its appearance, you will not be able to utilize that aspect. Radio ads can be expensive, though not as expensive as a TV ad.

- **Create a Website:** These days, almost everyone has a computer and surfs the World Wide Web. According to the United States Census, 75.6% of Americans reported living in a household that has a computer with Internet. With a marketing resource so accessible, not having a website seems like a travesty. Creating a website is an easy way to get your company out to the public. There are lots of places online that provide web hosting for under $50 a year. You will want to do some research to decide which company you want to host your site. Once that is complete, you want to contemplate creating your page. Creating a webpage that is functional is a big factor in setting up your website. You want to make sure it is easy for the consumer to use and navigate. The website needs to look clean and professional, and when people visit it, they should understand instantly what your product or service is.

  - **An About Us Page**- Give the public some insight on your company, your values and beliefs, and how you got started.
  - **Contact Us Page**- Here is a place you can provide your company address, phone number, emails, or a contact us box for customers to leave their information.
  - **A Product/Services Page**- This page could be to describe your services or product, or it could be the store to buy it from.
  - **FAQ**- Answer frequently asked questions that you get about your products or services in this area.

- **Social Media:** Over half of the population has a Facebook page or Twitter account. Consumers use social media to keep in touch with their friends, and smart businesses have learned how to adopt these sites to keep the customers engaged in their products. WebDAM reported that 52 percent of all marketers have found a customer via Facebook. They also reported that emails that include social media buttons have a click-through-rate 158 percent higher than emails that do not include social media buttons. A social media site can be used to post discount codes, news about the company, or just fun facts. Advertising is about getting the product and the company name/image to the consumer, and social media is a great avenue for that! Facebook, Twitter, and Instagram pages are basically free. You can pay extra to get additional advertising on the site, but if you build a big enough fan base, you will have all the social media advertising you need.

- **Networking Groups:** Networking is the exchange of information or services among individuals, groups, or institutions, specifically, the cultivation of productive relationships for employment or business. Networking groups are a great way to find better resources for your products, marketing, and advice. Networking groups have something in common, like being business owners. Sometimes a networking group can give or receive advice, discuss marketing strategies, or buy products.

Networking groups can increase your confidence in business. They can also help by providing connections and opportunities. While they are typically business oriented, networking groups can be a lot of fun. The group is considered to be like a "business social club." You can cultivate relationships with like-minded people, while boosting you and your company's names.

T I P #8

STRATEGIC STAFFING

 Back to a greater area of interest and expertise for me, Tip #8 asks you to avoid hiring mistakes with a strategic approach to staffing!

A lot of business owners believe they can't afford or don't have time to hire, don't know where to find people, and a bunch of other reasons that lead to hiring mistakes … perhaps the greatest hiring mistake of all is NOT hiring when the business NEEDS to hire!

A closely related mistake is "finally" hiring but doing so out of desperation of growing too fast or needing to stop the bleeding asap. When employers get "desperate" for help, they skip over basic hiring strategies that prevent hiring mistakes. The interview only asks two questions: Do you have a pulse? When can you start?

> ### KLOOBY SNACK
> the greatest hiring mistake of all is NOT hiring when the business NEEDS to hire!

Meanwhile, one of the greatest things I ever did for one of my favorite clients from 2011-2016 was coach him on my strategic staffing process and hold him accountable to hiring BEFORE he hit "desperation" … but barely!

At the time, he was accumulating a lot of work as an up-and-coming attorney. What he had learned about personal branding, networking, and marketing himself was working quite well—so well, in fact, he was getting nearly buried in case work. Being the only attorney in his firm, the work piled up, and he began to have a getting-home-for-dinner issue, as well as issues with customer service/punctuality, double booked appointments, missed due dates/deadlines, mistake-filled work, etc.

When it was predictable that he might lose clients, earn a bad reputation with judges or the community of attorneys, he agreed to let me coach him in the process summarized for you below. We can offer tons of coaching around each stage of the process and hope you approach us for any help you need in making great hires at the right time, while avoiding the common mistakes we most often see!

GET A KLU, INC.

STRATEGIC STAFFING PROCESS-OVERVIEW

The following describes the major steps in the Strategic Staffing Process. Get A Klu, Inc. can partner with your organization to provide some or all of the services described below.

OPEN REQUISITION:
- Clearly define each position in terms of: title, duties and qualifications required to perform those duties. Know where the position sits in an organizational chart.
- Clearly define the employment contract (major accountabilities) and compensation for each position.
- Establish Hiring Manager/Management and identify (secure approval to move forward from) all share-holders in the decision to hire.

RECRUITMENT AND SCREENING:
- Begin recruitment of candidates (methods include advertising, mining our own database of contacts for referrals, and postings on strategic job boards, and working with headhunting/agency partners).
- Applicants' resumes are then screened and categorized into "dismiss or pursue" based on experience and apparent skills, knowledge, abilities.
- Screening of applicants continues with a telephone interview that informs us of a candidate's:
  - Purposes for movements in their career (how they acquired/left previous positions and employers)
  - Current employment status and motivation in job search
  - Parameters or preferences for work location and environment or company culture
  - Salary history and expectations regarding future compensation and finally,
  - Desire to interview in person/on-site for the opportunity

INTEVIEWING AND SELECTION:
- On-site interviewing occurs in a minimum of two stages and in most cases three:
  - First on-site interview:
    - Candidate must answer "Competency-based" questions for which there is ONLY ONE RIGHT ANSWER.
    - If unable to successfully demonstrate competence, the interview is terminated at that time.
    - If the candidate demonstrates competence, the interview continues to "Behavioral/Situational" questions where candidates indicate how they would handle hypothetical situations that we can expect to come up in the course of performing the job they are interviewing for.
    - Candidate is then given the opportunity to ask questions about the opportunity, company, etc.
    - The first interview is concluded by asking if the candidate would like to officially apply for the position (i.e. complete full application, provide references and authorization to conduct credit and background checks, and agree to have behavioral and values assessments run on them).
  - Second on-site interview (selected from the most desired official applicants)
    - Share results of due diligence (credit, background and reference checks as well as the behavioral and values assessment results) with candidate.
    - Share the specific reasons why we are interested in moving forward with the candidate in balance with any concerns over needed areas of development, training or coaching that are predictable from the assessment results.
    - Share specifics regarding the compensation plan, expected hours of operation, performance/production standards, and possible start dates.
    - Verify candidate's interest and passion to join our team.
    - Extend Offer Letter and New Hire Paperwork.
  - Third on-site interview (if necessary)
    - This step is more of an orientation than an interview per se.
    - Time is taken to address any/all final concerns or issues to be worked through prior to start-date.
    - Establish and agree on specific start-date and preview the training, coaching and new-hire orientation schedules.

HIRE, ORIENTATION, TRAINING
- Announce and promote New Hire internally first, then externally to customers, clients, business and referral partners, etc.
- Begin Orientation, Training and Coaching programs early/asap relative to start date.

Get A Klu, Inc.

Get a Klu, Inc.
PO Box 720891
San Diego CA 92172

PHONE 619-405-3356
FAX   740-539-2346
E-MAIL info@getaklu.net

TIP #9

TRAINING FOR RETAINING

 The longer an employee stays with your company, the greater the ROI (return on investment) you get on the "cost of hire" for that employee. The greatest way to keep an employee for the long term is training, continual training, and additional training!

There is simply no point in hiring quality people if you do not provide them with quality training. Training is the best way to make sure your staff understands the company and their jobs. Having a team that knows the direction of the company and their working parts in that  company is always an asset. Let's explore what training your new employees should entail.

Teach Company Culture

What does the term "company culture" mean? Company culture is the behavior of the people in the company. The culture could be linked to the company's values, beliefs, goals, and more. Immersing your new employee in the culture of your business is one of the most important steps in training. Most companies briefly go over their culture during new employee orientations. An employee should understand their company's culture and be able to apply it while preforming their job functions. Providing the new recruit with a mentor who exemplifies the company culture is a great start. We also recommend that you provide your new hire with information, written or electronic, on your company culture.

Implement Actual Training for the Position

Training the new employee on the culture of the company is important, but you still have to train them for the job. The job description should help aid you in the training. Letting an employee know exactly what is expected of them is great but showing them is even better.

Most jobs are not A-B-C; they usually have multiple duties and functions. Making sure your new hire understands every facet of their job is a major factor in employee satisfaction and productivity. Training for the position should include written information and visually showing them how to complete their job tasks. Make sure to ask them questions to see if they understand.

Taking the time to show an employee the functions of their job shows them that you care and want them to have the tools they need to succeed. According to a survey done by ASTD in 2008, 65 percent of employees say the quality of training and learning opportunities positively influences their engagement.

Provide Feedback

You have hired great employees and trained them on the culture and their job duties. Now, you can sit back and do nothing, right? Wrong! This is the time to talk to your employees and provide them with feedback. Employees react to communication.

Most people want to do a good job and providing them with the feedback they need is imperative. This is an opportunity to praise them for doing a great job and correct any flaws in their performance. I know that the inclination is to praise but knowing what you are doing wrong is just as important as knowing what you're doing right.

When giving feedback, try to include a little positive and a little negative. Everyone has room for improvement.

Negative feedback is sometimes the hardest kind to give. As an employer, you want to keep your employees happy and content in their jobs. Here are some steps to make sure you are giving effective and constructive negative feedback:

- **Be Specific:** Make sure you are being very specific about what the employee needs to work on.
- **Explain the effects of the employee's actions:** Tell them why what they are doing is incorrect and how it affects the company, customer, or other employees.
- **Allow the employee to reply:** Give them a chance to reply to the information you have just given them. Ask questions to make sure they understand the error.
- **Provide resolution:** Tell them how to resolve the issue. Ask questions to make sure they understand.
- **Recap:** Review the information, stating what the error was, why, and what to do about it.
- **Remind them that you are in their corner:** Negative feedback is hard to hear sometimes but knowing that your supervisor is rooting for you makes it easier. Make sure they know you are trying to make them better, not tear them down.

Also, take this time to figure out if any adjustments need to be made in your training system. Providing your employees with the tools they need to succeed is the building block of a productive company filled with engaged employees.

Offer Additional Training, if Necessary

Sometimes errors or performance issues take more to fix than just talking. Additional training may be needed for some employees to optimize their job performance. When you train initially for a position, not every scenario presents itself in that two- or three-week window. As employees are cast off into the big company world, they might feel like they shouldn't ask questions. Offering additional training will allow your employees to gain new information, skills, and insight into their positions. This is also a great time to include items that you feel need to be revisited when you provided your feedback.

Having to retrain or give additional training to an employee does not make them a poor employee. An engaged and productive employee needs the tools to succeed; that is your job as an employer. It is truly important to make sure your employee knows that you are providing this training to boost them up, not bring them down.

Vipul and I love to help companies with their training initiatives. We dedicated a great deal of this tip to making sure an employee knows how to do their job. We also believe strongly in offering "soft skills" trainings for all members of a company, regardless of their job. Take a look at the following partial list of soft skills, and let us know if we can customize a workshop/training experience for your people in any of these areas:

Partial List: Soft-Skills Workshops/Trainings

- Anger Management
- Appreciative Inquiry
- Assertiveness and Self-Confidence
- Attention Management
- Being a Likeable Boss
- Business Acumen
- Business Ethics
- Business Succession Planning
- Change Management
- Civility in the Workplace
- Coaching and Mentoring
- Communication Strategies
- Conducting Annual Employee Reviews
- Conflict Resolution
- Creative Problem Solving
- Critical Thinking
- Customer Service
- Delivering Constructive Criticism
- Developing Corporate Behavior
- Developing New Managers
- Emotional Intelligence
- Employee Motivation
- Employee On-boarding
- Employee Recognition
- Facilitation Skills
- Generation Gaps
- Goal Setting and Getting Things Done
- High Performance Teams
- Hiring Strategies
- Human Resources Management
- Interpersonal Skills
- Knowledge Management
- Leadership and Influence
- Lean Process and Six Sigma
- Manager Management
- Managing Workplace Anxiety
- Meeting Management
- Middle Managers
- Millennial On-boarding
- Networking (in and outside of the Company)
- Office Politics for Managers
- Organizational Skills
- Performance Management
- Presentation Skills
- Project Management
- Proposal Writing
- Public Speaking
- Risk Assessment and Management
- Safety in the workplace
- Sales Fundamentals
- Social Intelligence
- Social Media in the Workplace
- Stress Management
- Supervising Others
- Talent Management
- Train the Trainer
- Virtual Team Building and Management
- Women in Leadership
- Work Life Balance

NOTE: Workshops and Trainings can be customized for ½ Day, Full Day or Multiple Day delivery schedules based on the breadth/depth of competence desired per subject. We work closely with Human Resources and Executive Teams to design the ideal curriculum for your learners.

T I P #10

BASIC GROWTH STRATEGIES

Assuming you have figured out what works in starting and running a business, the next step, or the last tip in this section, is to grow the business. Earlier, we mentioned that if you are not growing, you are dying! Many entrepreneurs make the mistake of over-celebrating "growing" a successful business by failing to continually plan for continuous growth! This section concludes by suggesting you always have a plan to grow your business.

Offer More Products / Services

This is a relatively simple way to grow what you already run. For example, if you own a pizza shop that strictly sells pizza, consider adding something to complement the pizza—say, chicken wings. The key to determining your new offerings is deciding if it is something that your current customer base wants. You can informally ask customers for feedback as they frequent the shop or ask them to complete a questionnaire, providing their thoughts. If the new product is something that will attract a new customer base, decide if there is currently a market for the product and if you're willing to aggressively promote the product so pursuing it is worthwhile.

Open Another Location

Even though it is a lot more complex than just adding new products, opening an additional store or place of business can produce positive results. In some ways, opening a new location is like starting from scratch.

You must:

- Determine the location. We've all heard it: Location! Location! Location! This is especially true when adding on to an existing business. The purpose for expanding your business this way is to drastically increase profits. You want to get the most out of this investment, so do your homework on the most beneficial location.
- Hire and/or train employees.
- Set up shop. Stock the business with your products and make other preparations for opening day.
- Promote the new products / services.

Franchise Opportunities

Choosing to franchise your business is a serious commitment, so carefully think through what you hope to achieve by franchising and determine if this is something you can accomplish by opening additional branches of your company or if franchising is truly the answer. One of the main differences between franchising vs. opening an additional location is that with franchising, the franchisee would be responsible for providing the capital to start, run, and grow the business, while it would be your task if you select to open an additional location.

If you agree franchising is what your company needs to do to capture additional market share, consider these things:

- You need to understand your company. It seems that you should already "understand your company" by now, but you don't realize you don't really know your company until someone asks you a question about it that you cannot answer. As the franchisor, you are the main representative of the company, and before you attract franchisees, you need to be able to describe to them the benefits of franchising with your company, rather than going to your competition.
- What does this mean legally? Consult a professional for help with deciphering the laws surrounding franchising. Doing so early on can help avoid legal woes in the future.

- Set the guidelines for the candidates wanting to become your franchisees.
- Screen and select franchisees.

Scoring Large Contracts

Acquiring contracts to provide your products and/or services to other organizations can be a great benefit to your company. You may be approached by a company asking you to be their supplier, but that's not likely. Typically, you will have to seek these contracts. Some companies advertise contract opportunities on their websites. Each has a set method of how to apply for the opportunity. Some require that you just complete an application, while others might require an application, formal bid proposal, and accompanying documentation, such as a capability statement.

Elements of a Winning Proposal

- Name of your company
- Background of your company (e.g., when formed, financial info, etc.)
- Your company's mission statement
- Products and/or services your company offers and how long for each
- Previous clients

Before bidding on these contracts, you must ensure your company is fit to deliver. Some basic questions to ask yourself to gauge how ready you truly are include:

- Do I have the financial and personnel resources to fulfill the contract?
- Are the company's needs in line with what my company offers?

As with all the tips, we stop short of covering all that can be covered … hopefully, providing enough for you to do the rest and apply these to your business.

The basic time-tested and true methods we have summarized above can be offered without knowing anything about your business. And the more we know about any business, the more creative we can get about ways to grow. Vipul and I love getting creative or resourceful in helping proven businesses expand and grow. We hope you'll consider 2 complimentary sessions with us to learn about your business and explore growth opportunities together!

LEADERSHIP AND INFLUENCE

T I P #1

ONE SIZE DOES NOT FIT ALL!

Very simply, we have seen that there are a variety of attributes and abilities associated with leadership, and these vary from leader to leader. Some leaders are great orators; others great are writers. Some leaders are very quiet, but the force of their logic or passion wins the day.

The difference between a good leader and a great leader is partly the number of leadership skills you have developed. The other part is your ability to apply those skills properly to those who would follow.

Developing and applying leadership skills is the subject of upcoming tips, while this first tip is a basic "heads up" on characteristics, principles, and styles that are most/commonly associated with leaders ... toward helping you decide what kind of leader you want to be!

Characteristics of a Leader

The mark of a true leader is not a position or title, but it is how many people are willing to follow them. Santa Clara University and the Tom Peters Group outline the following leadership characteristics.

Which of these do you know you already possess? Which of these would OTHERS use in their description of you as a person or leader? Which of these is a "missing" for you in your leadership style or effectiveness?

- Honest
- Forward-looking
- Competent
- Inspiring
- Intelligent
- Fair-minded
- Broad-minded
- Supportive
- Straightforward
- Dependable
- Cooperative
- Determined
- Imaginative
- Ambitious
- Courageous
- Caring
- Mature
- Loyal
- Self-controlled
- Independent

Leadership Principles

We looked no further than The United States Army for these 11 leadership principles. Which of these do you already follow? Which of these is a "missing" for your desired style (and effectiveness) as a leader?

- Be tactically and technically proficient
- Know yourself and seek self-improvement
- Know your soldiers and look out for their welfare
- Keep your soldiers informed
- Set the example
- Ensure the task is understood, supervised, and accomplished
- Train your soldiers as a team

- Make sound and timely decisions

- Develop a sense of responsibility in your subordinates

- Employ your unit in accordance with its capabilities

- Seek responsibility and take responsibility for your actions

(Situational) Leadership Styles

Now we get to the nuts and bolts of leadership. The definitive leadership style research comes from Paul Hersey and Kenneth Blanchard, which they expressed in their Situational Leadership Model. The Hersey-Blanchard model addresses the key to practical leadership development: the attributes and styles of the *followers*.

Not everyone is on the same intellectual, maturity, compliance, or motivational level. Different people are motivated by different things, and this must be taken into account if one is to be a great leader.

Communications experts, myself inKLUded, consider it critical to tailor your message to your "target audience." It is the followers that you want to motivate and influence, and you cannot do that if you don't know whom you are trying to motivate or influence.

The Situational Leadership model addresses four types of leadership styles, based on the follower:

- Telling
- Selling
- Participating
- Delegating

The goal is to develop followers to the delegating level as seen in the illustration on the next page:

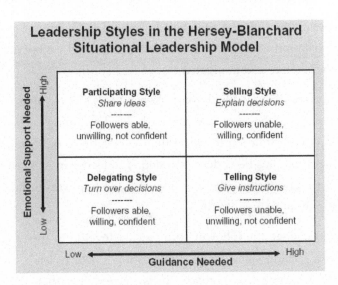

Leadership Styles in the Hersey-Blanchard Situational Leadership Model

	Low ← Guidance Needed → High
High Emotional Support Needed **Low**	**Participating Style** *Share ideas* ---- Followers able, unwilling, not confident **Selling Style** *Explain decisions* ---- Followers unable, willing, confident
	Delegating Style *Turn over decisions* ---- Followers able, willing, confident **Telling Style** *Give instructions* ---- Followers unable, unwilling, not confident

Situational Leadership: Telling

Telling is the lowest level of leadership style. Most new employees require direct instructions, so this is called the "Telling" or "Directing" style. The follower is characterized by low competence and high commitment, being unable to comply, with possible feelings of insecurity.

The leader must focus highly on tasks, rather than a relationship with the employee, as a relationship does not yet exist.

When an employee can't do the job because they are unknowledgeable, the leader must spend much more time working with the employee, offering clear instructions and regular follow up.

The leader must be encouraging and motivational, offering praise for positive results and correction for less than positive results. The idea is to motivate the follower to rise to the next level of ability.

This is a very leader-driven stage.

Situational Leadership: Selling

Selling addresses the follower who has developed some competence with an improved commitment. The follower is not convinced yet but is open to becoming cooperative and motivated.

The leader must still focus highly on tasks, and this still requires much of the leader's time, but the focus now also includes developing a relationship with the employee. Build on the trust that has begun to develop and the encouragement that has been demonstrated. The leader must spend more time listening and offering advice, scheduling the follower for additional training if the situation requires it.

The goal is to engage the follower so they can develop to the next level. There is less "telling" and more "suggesting," which leads to more encouragement, acting as a coach. It is recognition that they have progressed and motivates them to progress even further.

This is a very leader-driven stage.

Situational Leadership: Participating

Participating addresses the follower who is now competent at the job but remains somewhat inconsistent and is not yet fully committed. The follower may be uncooperative or performing as little work as possible, despite their competence with the tasks. The leader must participate with and support the follower.

The leader no longer needs to give detailed instructions and follow up as often, but he/she does need to continue working with the follower to ensure the work is being done at the level required.

The follower is now highly competent but is not yet convinced in his or her ability or fully committed to do their best and excel. The leader must now focus less on the tasks assigned and more on the relationship between the follower, the leader, and the group.

This is a very follower-driven, relationship-focused stage.

Situational Leadership: Delegating

Delegating is the ultimate goal: a follower who feels fully empowered and competent enough to take the ball and run with it, with minimal supervision. The follower is highly competent, highly committed, motivated, and empowered.

The leader can now delegate tasks to the follower and observe with minimal follow up, knowing that acceptable or even excellent results will be achieved. There is a low focus on tasks and on relationships. There is no need to compliment the follower on every task, although continued praise for outstanding performance must be given as appropriate.

This is a very follower-driven stage.

In Summary

You will notice that none of the above actually tells you *how to lead* in a practical manner. They don't address what to do or say in any given situation. That is because there is no real formula to being a leader.

We believe that leadership must come from within, and it is based on your personality.

In the tips that follow, you will learn how to develop your innate leadership abilities and build the confidence required in being a true leader.

What we want for you to get out of THIS tip is to have an to have an answer if asked, "What kind of leader are you?" or "What are your greatest leadership qualities?"

T I P #2

LEADERS LOOK WITHIN

 We organize this tip with two prompting questions and ask you to DO the soul-searching for the time and discipline to arrive at your very best answers:

- As a leader, what are you able and willing to *DO for others* in order to become a better leader?
- As a leader, what are you able and willing to *DO for yourself* in order to become a better leader?

For Others:

James Kouzes and Barry Posner asked thousands of people to rank a list of characteristics associated with leadership, including the seven top qualities that motivated them to follow willingly. They gave this survey to over 75,000 people over a 20-year period, and the authors identified five abilities that were crucial to successful leadership:

- **Model the Way:** You must lead by example. You can't come into work 10 minutes late every day if you want your employees to arrive on time. We'll elaborate in Tip #3!

- **Inspire a Shared Vision:** If you capture the imagination, you will inspire creative thought and increase loyalty. The vision doesn't need to be grandiose, but it needs to be communicated effectively for others to adopt it as their own. We'll elaborate in Tip #4!

- **Challenge the Process**: Don't continue doing something just because "We've always done it that way." Situations change, and sometimes there is a policy or procedure that never worked well in the first place. Think outside the box. We'll elaborate in Tip #5!

- **Enable Others to Act**: Truly empower people to act on their own within their level of authority. The famed Ritz-Carlton Hotel empowers every employee at all levels to spend up to $1,000 on behalf of a guest (who is informed reimbursement will be required for whatever request they make). We'll elaborate in Tip #6!

- **Encourage the Heart**: A positive attitude is infectious. If the leader appears passionate or excited about the vision, others will catch the enthusiasm, as well. We'll elaborate in Tip #7!

For Yourself:

Now that Tip #1 covered the basics, it's time to assess or plan how you are incorporating them into your life/businesses.

Set Leadership Goals: In leadership, as in life, you will never come to the end of your learning, but you want to rank in priority order those qualities you want to develop. We will dedicate Tip #8 to "S.M.A.A.R.T." Goal Setting.

Address the Goals: Determine how you will accomplish your goals. Do you feel you need to learn more about teamwork so you can better lead a team? Join a team sport. Do you want to communicate better or feel more comfortable in social situations? Take a creative writing class or join Toastmasters and get some public speaking experience.

Seek Inspiration: Learn about a variety of leaders, including their styles with dealing with challenges. Read books and conduct research on the Internet or at libraries. It is always a possibility that you, as a leader, will be asked who you look up to as a leader, and you will always want to have strong/relevant/honest answers without any pauses or guesswork.

Choose a Role Model: Based on your research, choose a role model that fits your personality. You might choose a dynamic leader like Teddy Roosevelt or an intellectual leader like Albert Schweitzer or Albert Einstein. Read several biographies and find videos on his or her life. Michael Jordan and Muhammad Ali, respectively, are among the role models for me and Vipul.

Seek Experience: Take a leadership role in a social group or club. Gain experience working with people on many levels. Vipul and I have learned a lot about leadership when volunteering in youth sports organizations. There is always a healthy amount of politics to learn from when parents are volunteering to be leaders for the community's children! We digress! ☺

Create a Personal Mission Statement: Imagine your legacy. How do you want to be remembered? What do you want people to think of you? What type of leader are you determined to be? Write a statement that defines who you will become.

Vipul and I would LOVE the opportunity to be sources of accountability for the things we recommend you do so you are able to do the things effective leaders do for others!

T I P #3

TO HAVE AND TO BE A MODEL!

In the last tip, we only briefly touched on the suggestion of choosing role models. This tip goes deeper by encouraging you to BE a role model. In deciding what leadership qualities you most wish to model for others, you will calibrate your ideas of what role models will be right for yourself.

Remember that the best leaders are examples of what they want their followers to be. George Washington rode into battle with his troops. You cannot lead from the rear and send your followers out to take the heat and face the challenges. If you remain in an ivory tower, it will eliminate any possibility of respect.

By definition, a leader is in the *lead*, right up front, ready to take the heat if something goes wrong. If something does go wrong, a true leader never blames his followers, even if, in fact, they failed. A true leader takes the blame and then addresses how to correct the problems that arose.

Determining Your Way

Once you have chosen your role model, study what qualities made them successful. Learn about the challenges they faced and how the challenges were met. Learn about the ideas and philosophies that drove them and made them successful. Study again the Hersey- Blanchard model and see how different situations called for different styles of leadership.

Since there is no leader in history who has not had failures, pay particular attention to how your hero deals with adversity. George Washington nearly lost the American Revolution through major hesitations in leadership, and, in fact, he lost New York to the British general William Howe, but he learned from his mistakes, and the rest, as they say, is history.

Being an Inspirational Role Model

Leadership is neither for the timid nor for the arrogant. That said, confidence is often resented or misinterpreted for arrogance.

People who lack self-confidence often feel intimidated by a true leader. This should never hold you back. If you have honesty, integrity, and deal with everyone fairly, others will see that. Be willing to listen to criticism, but also consider the source.

If you are too afraid of what others might say about you, or you ignore legitimate complaints and insist on respect solely because of your position, you will lose the respect and cooperation of your followers and peers.

President Theodore Roosevelt may have said it best:

 *"It is not the critic who counts; not the man who points out how the strong man stumbles, or where the doer of deeds could have done them better. The credit belongs to the man who is actually in the arena, whose face is marred by dust and sweat and blood, who strives valiantly; who errs and comes short again and again; because there is not effort without error and shortcomings; but who does actually strive to do the deed; who knows the great enthusiasm, the great devotion, who spends himself in a worthy cause, who at the best knows in the end the triumph of high achievement and who at the worst, if he fails, at least he fails while daring greatly. So that his place shall never be with those cold and timid souls who know neither victory nor defeat."*

Influencing Others' Perspectives

You may have heard that perception is reality. You must always present an honest, caring, dedicated attitude to inspire others. To inspire loyalty, you must have a track record of honesty and fairness. If any of your followers feel they have been wronged, for whatever reason, you need to address the issue immediately. People talk, and a problem ignored is a problem that grows.

Believe it or not, the most powerful influence you can have is often not trying to influence someone. When people believe you are open to their suggestions and believe they have been heard, they will work harder, even if they disagree with the methods or goals. Simply listening to others makes them feel empowered, even if you don't accept their suggestions.

If a follower feels there's no point in talking to you, they won't, and they will disengage themselves from your vision and will follow your directions begrudgingly.

If you are seen as going the extra mile, your followers are more likely to go the extra mile. If you hide in your office and people never see you, you will be perceived as out of the loop, uninformed, uninterested, and, therefore, unworthy to lead.

Many a successful corporate executive makes it a point to be seen by their employees every day. If an employee is to be commended for something, it is done publicly, often right in the middle of their workplace while they are surrounded by their coworkers. That sends a powerful message to everyone.

TIP #4

DEFINE AND SELL YOUR VISION

 Ask yourself the following question: What do I want (for any area of your life, but mostly for the areas where you expect or are expected to lead)? What do you want? What do you REALLY, REALLY want?

Now, keeping that question in mind, close your eyes and "look out" as far ahead into the future as you can possibly see … further … further … now, what do you see?

> KLOOBY SNACK
> Your vision is a description of the "way things are" as far into the future as you can imagine.

Your responses to the exercise/questions above make up your vision! Simply put, what do you see when you look out as far as you can see?

People often confuse vision with mission. In our opinion, a mission is the greatest milestone (accomplishment, achievement, destination, triumph, etc.) we can imagine "getting to" on the way to our vision. The vision is a description of the "way things are" as far into the future as we can imagine.

Finally, objectives is the term Vipul and I use for an annual timeframe. Every year, there are major objectives that guide our progress toward a mission, which, when accomplished, proves we are on the right track toward our vision. From there, as we will discuss in its own tip, we look to a quarterly timeframe for S.M.A.A.R.T. goal setting.

Humor us while we give a basic example:

Vision (farthest out we can see): The USA will be the global leader among all countries committed to space exploration!

Mission (could be several years out): By the end of the decade, we will land a human being on the moon with safe return to Earth.

Objective (annual): This year, our objectives are to secure funding from Congress, select the team of astronauts that will fly Apollo Project spacecrafts, and begin design on spacesuit upgrades required for the lunar surface. (I am making this up, of course, but you get the idea.)

Many leaders (entrepreneurs/owners) make the mistake of writing mission statements, values statements, and company objectives and even engage in company-wide and departmental goal setting WITHOUT ever having gotten clear on the vision!

When you can get super clear on your vision and then SELL it to your people, everything else that guides engagement and productivity is so much easier!

Communicating Your Vision

Communication is more than just the words you say or the memos you write. Remember, actions speak louder than words. Take every opportunity to communicate your vision in words and deeds. One of the best ways to communicate a vision is to sum it up in a simple catch phrase.

Post your slogan, catch phrase, and mission statement in prominent locations. When you send emails, list it in quotes below your signature block. Hold meetings occasionally or hand out "Visionary Awards" to people who exemplify your vision. Above all, lead by example.

Identifying the Benefit for Others

Answer the question, "What's in it for me?" as if you were one of your own followers. The answer might not always be obvious. Certainly, performance bonuses and awards work, but most followers enjoy being part of a larger, successful organization.

Everyone loves a winner. When the home team wins at the stadium, you would think the fans in the stand were the players by the way they share in the victory and excitement.

We are social creatures who like to feel we belong. We crave acceptance. If you can get your followers to accept your vision as their own, and excite them about being part of it, they will often excel beyond what you (or they) thought possible. Be sure to reward loyalty and performance above and beyond the call of duty.

Please show up for our weekly tip reading to ask Vipul and I to discuss our individual and shared visions. This book is a bit of a milestone for our vision of working together. We love to talk about the future and what it will take to get there, namely, selling the future you see to the people you'll be leading!

T I P #5

CHALLENGE THE STATUS QUO

 Far too often, we cling to what is familiar, even if we know it to be inadequate. Most large groups are governed by the law of inertia: if it takes effort to change something, nothing will change. As a leader, you must search for opportunities to change, grow, innovate, and improve.

There is no reward without risk, however; so you must be willing to experiment, take risks, and learn from mistakes. Ask questions, even if you fear the answers. Start with the question, "Why?" Why are things the way they are? Why do we do things the way we do?

Think Outside the Box

A *paradigm* is an established model or structure. Sometimes they work quite  well, but often they are inadequate or even counterproductive. Sometimes it is necessary to "think outside the box" and break the paradigm. Don't be afraid to ask questions of your followers, employees, customers, former leaders. Answers and ideas can be found in the least likely places. Often the lowest ranking persons in an organization can tell you exactly what is wrong because they see it daily from their vantage points.

Developing Your Inner Innovator

Innovation is more than just improvement on a process or procedure; it is a total redirection or restructuring based upon stated goals and research.

While it can be helpful to adapt an outdated procedure or task to today's standards, often the procedure itself is the problem, not the manner in which it is implemented. Innovators reverse engineer policies and procedures based on the new vision and goals, working from the target backwards, rather than from the status quo looking forward.

To be sure, not all innovative strategies will be feasible or cost effective. Requiring an entirely new computerized network and infrastructure, for example, may cost hundreds of thousands of dollars and produce little improved efficiency. However, if you don't start thinking "outside the box," you will miss many valuable solutions that can and will work.

Note that change should never be made simply for the sake of change. Change can be exciting, but it can also be unnerving and difficult for employees. Constant change causes frustration. Moreover, if you seem to change too many things too often, you will lose respect, as your followers perceive you don't really know what you are doing, so plan your innovations carefully. There should be solid evidence that a new way of doing things is likely to work before you invest money and everyone's time.

Keep focused on the goals and be willing to break the rules if they need to be broken. Just make sure they really need to be broken and you don't break something that needs to keep working! With proper research and planning, you can dare to be bold!

Seeing Room for Improvement

A strong vision does not lend itself to mediocrity. A drive to excellence always seeks improvement. If you accept 95% efficiency as a goal, the efficiency will inevitably slip to 90%. If that's considered "good enough," it will become hard to keep it above 85% and so on. A vision is a goal that is strived to achieve.

Goals must not be unrealistic or unattainable, or the followers will simply give up trying altogether, becoming dispirited and demoralized in the process. If 95% of people fail to meet a standard, that standard is likely too high and must be changed. On the other hand, the bar must not be set so low that little or no effort is required to meet it.

Based on your vision, set high goals that are attainable but with some degree of difficulty, and reward those who meet the goals. If a large number of followers are meeting the goal, raise the target. If only a very few are meeting it, lower it somewhat.

Investigate any potential bottlenecks that might be stifling progress and resolve them. Talk to your followers about possible solutions. The people who actually do the work are far more likely to be able to tell you why they are having difficulty accomplishing a task than their supervisors.

Lobbying for Change

To lobby for change, you need to influence people and excite them about your vision. You may need to persuade a reluctant boss or fight a corporate culture that doesn't understand what you are trying to do. In that case, you need to demonstrate why your requested change needs to occur.

Do your research, and always enter a meeting prepared. Study the situation and present all of your findings in a short report, preferably with simple charts or graphs. Have the details ready in case you are asked a question, but don't overload people with facts. Show as clearly as possible how your plan will effect positive change.

If you are lobbying your own followers, the same is true. You may want to revolutionize a cultural change. Perhaps you are a shop manager and people are unmotivated. You may need to bring about change slowly, rather than with one big dramatic gesture. On the other hand, you may need to shake things up in a big way. Whatever the situation, you can successfully lobby for change if you attack the problem with a plan, sound reasoning, and infectious enthusiasm!

T I P #6

(POSITIVELY) ENABLING OTHERS

Most of the time, we use (or hear) the term "enabler" in reference to the person who "allows, fails to interrupt/prevent, or even encourages" a negative or destructive behavior. We want that, but for positive, constructive, productive behaviors! Simply put, we do want you to be an enabler … but the good kind! ☺

As mentioned before, you cannot do your followers' work for them. Besides, if you do their work, what are they getting paid for? You have your own work to do. This is the ultimate goal of the Hersey-Blanchard situational Leadership model: to develop your followers to the point where you can delegate tasks without a lot of oversight.

> **KLOOBY SNACK**
>
> Simply put, we DO want you to be an enabler … but the good kind!

To be a true leader, you must enable others to act responsibly and not encourage bad worker habits by compensating for them or overlooking them. At the same time, you cannot berate a follower for trying hard but making an honest mistake. The goal of a leader is to empower others to work. The extent that you can do this is the extent that you will be successful.

Encouraging Growth in Others

A positive attitude is essential to encouragement. No one likes to fail, and many take it very personally. While failure should never be rewarded, an understanding attitude and positive outlook can work wonders. A child only learns to walk by falling down many times. The focus is not on the fall, but on getting up. The goal is to walk … then to run.

Meeting with an employee one-on-one is important to positive motivation. Again, you must use the power of listening. Avoid blame when something goes wrong and focus on the reason for the failure. You might learn someone needs more training, more self-confidence, or more freedom. You might learn someone does not have the tools needed to be successful. You will never know if you don't ask questions and listen – or worse, if you berate someone for a failure.

If someone is willfully defiant, then feel free to be stern and resolute. Take disciplinary action if necessary and document the conversation. If you allow someone to be defiant or lazy out of a misplaced concern for his or her feelings, you will be performing a great injustice against the rest who are working hard. In most cases, people really do want to do a good job, and they have a sense of pride when they meet a challenge.

Creating Mutual Respect

You will never be worthy of respect if you don't give respect. Respect should be given to everyone at all levels, unless they deliberately do something to lose that respect.

You need to build respect in other ways, as well. Be visible to your followers. Show them you are available and interested in knowing everything they do. Develop and demonstrate your knowledge of the organization and details of the product, service, or operation. If you are perceived as being knowledgeable and can answer questions, you will not only earn respect, but will motivate others to learn, as well.

The Importance of Trust

Respect inevitably leads to trust. Do what you say and say what you mean. Under-promise and over-deliver can help manage expectations. If you are given a task you know will take you one hour, say you "should" have it done in two hours. You never know when you'll get a phone call that eats into your time or when an emergency may pop up. If you get done in less than two hours, you will be perceived as a hero. If not, you can call and apologize that it will be "a little later" without much trouble because you said you *should* have it done. You didn't promise that you *would* have it done. If people feel they can rely on you, they will trust you.

Also, let people know that you are not asking them to do anything you would not do yourself, or that you haven't done in the past. Work hard and be seen working hard. If you come in early and see others who are there early, as well, stop by and simply mention that fact positively. A simple word of recognition will go a long way to earning respect. Without respect, you will never have loyalty; and without loyalty, you cannot trust your followers. Without mutual trust and respect, you cannot accomplish great things.

Remember, while your people need to be able to trust you, you need to build them up to the level where you can also trust them. Also remember that this book is a collection of tips, not a complete training. We want you to ask us about our library of soft skills trainings for leaders who wish to master the skills of trust building and more!

TIP #7

BOTTOM OF HEART IS BOTTOM LINE!

Employees, workers, and followers are not robots. Human beings have intellect and emotions. Failing to deal with them on those levels will ultimately backfire. You cannot program loyalty. If your leadership recognizes the heartbeat of the business, its people, more engagement will lead to greater achievement and a healthier bottom line.

Here are very basic ideas on touching the hearts of your people.

Sharing Rewards

If your followers are going to share in the work, make certain they share in the rewards. If you are going to get a bonus for a successful task, share at least a portion of it with your followers.

More than one employee has felt betrayed by leadership when the boss gets a big bonus and those who do all the work get nothing. You don't need to give them half or divide it all up among all your followers, but you should at least throw them a party, provide a free lunch, or give everyone a pair of movie tickets or a lottery ticket. Do something to show they didn't work hard only to see you take all the credit.

Celebrating Accomplishments

Set both personal and team goals and milestones. Nothing motivates someone like public recognition. Although some may seem somewhat embarrassed by a public display, inside they are proud they have been recognized.

Celebrate team milestones, as well. It breaks up the routine of the workday, gives a well-deserved break, and motivates people to work harder when they return to work refreshed.

Making Celebration Part of Your Culture

 You don't need to decorate the office every day or have morning pep rallies, but the workplace should never be dreaded by employees. People spend most of their waking lives at work, with substantially less time for their family, friends, and activities they would much rather be doing. By definition, they come to "work," and you have to pay them to be there. People want to feel incentivized by more than just a paycheck.

Be sure to have a welcoming environment where people feel respected. Celebrate special occasions to break up the routine, but don't make celebration itself the routine or no work will get done.

T I P #8

SMAART GOAL SETTING

 Tip #3 from the Accountability section of the first edition of *Get A Klu in 52* is reprinted here—get this, with permission from myself.☺

We already mentioned (in Tip #4 of this section) that a **Goal** is the quarterly "what by when" that gets set from the (annual) **Objectives** that must be met on the way to achieving a long-term **Mission** on the way to realizing the ultimate **Vision!**

You are about to read an explanation of how and why I added an "A" and changed the "R" in the original "SMART" model that everyone learns in goal setting. Stay with us on this one and consider letting Vipul and I "calibrate" your goals to the S.M.A.A.R.T. criteria we are about to explain.

GET S.M.A.A.R.T. ABOUT GOAL SETTING!

As with integrity, when asked, most people will tell you that they set goals. This is because they are confusing a hope, wish, dream (macro) or a task, activity, or commitment (micro) with a goal. Second, most people are unaware how vast the studies are that have been conducted on high-achieving individuals that reveal 100% of them to share the habit of goal setting, but also tell us that only 3% of the population sets goals.

When I speak and train clients on goal setting, I make sure people understand the five reasons why we fail to set goals, and one of those is that we don't know how. I personally never learned how to set goals in school, which was bad enough, but then when I finally did learn about goals during my coaches training education, I learned to make goals S.M.A.R.T. (specific, measurable, achievable, realistic, and time-bound), in turn, making them accountable. I was thrilled!

What a difference when we add "specific, measurable, and time-bound" as criteria to what we want—that's the difference between a hope, wish, dream, and a GOAL: a specific and measurable "what" happens by a specific time-bound "when."

> **KLOOBY SNACK**
>
> The difference between a hope, wish, or dream and a GOAL: A goal is specific and measurable "what" happens by a specific time-bound "when."

But there's more to the model (the "A" and the "R") and soon into building my own coaching practice, I realized there was something stupid about S.M.A.R.T. ... just kidding ... I mean, there was something redundant and a couple things missing. Let me explain...

The original "A" is for "achievable or attainable" and one way to know that our goals are achievable is if we *believe* we can achieve them. Belief is a feeling of certainty that something is true ... so if we believe we can do it then that becomes our reality: we can do it! Therefore, if the goal is achievable (we believe we can and that's our reality) then it is also realistic (to us) and that makes the "R" in S.M.A.R.T. redundant.

Are you tracking? When I am helping clients set goals, I hold them accountable to ONLY setting a goal they truly believe they can achieve— not the goal they know they are going to achieve no matter what, but the one they know the CAN achieve even if it will be difficult or require effort! Hold that thought ...(Visit www.theklubrary.com for free and for-pay content, including real life samples of me coaching people on goal setting). Meanwhile...

Another problem I saw in the model were two things I felt were missing:

1) ambition/will-power, and 2) motivation or the "why" of the goal!

Meaning, with the original S.M.A.R.T. criteria, someone could set a goal to achieve something predictable, or that they are already going to achieve anyway and think it's a goal. Meaning, someone could set a goal that meets the S.M.A.R.T. criteria without having to change behavior. Someone could set a goal of brushing their teeth twice a day for 30 days straight—something they are likely to do anyway, whether they call it a goal or not.

In the coaching business, we are interested in helping people get results they DON'T already have, which means they need to change behavior in some way, and if so, then their goal is ambitious. The second "A" in my model is for the "ambition" it takes to decrease, increase, start, or stop a behavior, but doing the same thing over and over expecting different results, as we all know, is insanity! So, when it comes to goal setting, make sure you are aware of a behavior that needs to change in order for the goal to be achieved ... or it's not really a goal, is it?

What about the "R" then? The original S.M.A.R.T. model uses "R" for realistic, which I think is redundant, but also leaves "why" or "motivation" out of the model. So, I changed the "R" from realistic (which we established is covered by "achievable") to "reason/reward," because, in the words of Simon Sinek, it is critical to "Know Your Why." When I work with my coaching clients to set goals, I hold them accountable to declaring as much "WHY they want the goal" as possible. (Visit www.theklubrary.com for free and affordable e-sources and e- courses.) They need to have more reasons to want to achieve the goal than to give up on or procrastinate on it. If we have just one reason for doing something, we might get around to doing it. But if we are clear on five or six reasons why we want something, we might be unstoppable and certainly more willing to be held accountable!

I would like to think I have made S.M.A.R.T. even S.M.A.A.R.T.er ... and to make it even S.M.A.A.R.T.E.R., you add the "E" for evaluate ... and the second "R" for revise. My mom taught me that humans plan and God laughs. Therefore, it is important to periodically check in on the progress you are making or make room for unexpected life events and evaluate/revise your goals to make sure they are always achievable and relevant.

If you'd like to get S.M.A.A.R.T. about your own goal setting, consider sessions with a Get A Klu coach or the self-paced e-course on SMAART Goal Setting I recorded. (Visit www.theklubrary.com for free and affordable e-sources and e-courses.) Learn it! Live it!

Jeff Klubeck loves conducting Goal-Setting Workshops, where NO whiteboard is safe!

T I P #9

INGREDIENTS OF PERSUASION

This first of two tips on persuasion will close out this section. First, we'll break down what I call the "ingredients" of persuasion ... never try to cook a persuasive meal without one, two, or IDEALLY all three of the ingredients below.

In the next and last tip, we'll summarize "instructions" of persuasion ... various steps you can take to BE persuasive ... again, being sure to use at least one, if not all three, of the following ingredients!

The Ingredients of Persuasion

Aristotle was a master of the art persuasion, and he outlines his thinking in his work, Rhetoric, where he identifies three important factors (that I refer to as Ingredients of Persuasion): logos, ethos, and pathos.

- **Logos** (logical) persuades people by appealing to their intellect. This was Aristotle's favorite and his forte', but not everyone reacts on a rational level. Appealing to intellect is more than telling someone they are smart and expecting that to persuade them. By appealing to intellect, we mean "using logical argument" to persuade. An argument is a claim statement that is supported by evidence and reasoning. Sometimes, the argument alone is all that is needed to be persuasive.

- **Ethos** (credibility) persuades people using character. Your character convinces the follower that you are someone who is worth listening to for advice. Sometimes, the "strength" of the argument (the claim is true, and both the evidence and reasoning are "logical") is enough to make someone credible. Other times, we need to know a track record, achievement, certification, license, or level of experience to determine if someone is credible or not. Work hard to understand what makes someone credible and strive to communicate your credibility for the arguments you are making. Said another way, the argument is what you know ... your credibility is HOW you know what you know!

- **Pathos** (emotional) persuades people by appealing to their emotions. For example, when a politician wants to gain support for a bill, it inevitably is argued, "It's for the children!" Babies, puppies, and kitties abound in advertising for a reason. Cars are sometimes called "sexy" in car commercials. Pathos allows you to tie into emotional triggers that will capture a person's attention and enlist their support, but it can be easily abused, leading to a loss of ethos, as described above.

The truth is that each of these ingredients can be abused, distorted, misplaced, or misrepresented. Celebrities are paid lots of money to endorse products like cars or insurance—"fame and popularity" get mistaken for true credibility. An appeal to an emotion may be accurate when the argument being presented with that appeal is patently false.

We are being very brief in this tip in simply suggesting that if you intend to be persuasive, we recommend getting very clear on the arguments you'll be making ... your credibility in making those arguments and what emotions you'll be appealing to in order to be as effective as possible in your efforts.

First things first...or last thing last...the next tip is the last in this section; it covers some approaches (armed with the above three ingredients) to being persuasive.

> I was a Professor of Public Speaking for 20 consecutive years and have since had "Speaker Coaching" assignments with entrepreneurs in 12 countries over the past 5 years. I have literally helped hundreds of people, including Vipul, write and deliver persuasive speeches, and I would really love to work with you, too!

T I P #10
INSTRUCTIONS FOR PERSUASION

 As simply as I can possibly state it, here are your instructions for being persuasive:

- Define the Issue (issue = problem/opportunity).

- Illuminate the Barriers to Resolving the Issue (internal and external ... structural and attitudinal).

- Propose Solutions (do-able, observable actions you want your audience to take that address the barriers and resolve the issue).

That's the simplicity of it. While you are doing the three things above, you'll want to include your ingredients: Logos, Ethos and Pathos.

And, as a gift to you, we'll close out this tip and section on leadership and influence by supplying an outline template that I use in my Eight Steps to Fearless Public Speaking course.

The step-by-step guide to planning a persuasive speech is an excerpt from my e-book: *8 Steps to Fearless Public Speaking*. It is "skeletal" in nature so we know it may create as many or more questions for you than it will answer ... that is because we hope it motivates you to schedule a couple coaching sessions with us to see how we can get your vision or mission (or sales pitch) into persuasive speech form!

GET THEM TO TAKE ACTION! PLANNING A PERSUASIVE/SALES PRESENTATION

I. Introduction ("tell 'em what you are going to tell 'em!"...remember that this is an intro, so be efficient here!)

    A. Gather Attention: (story, quote, joke, or ask a relevant/interactive question)

    B. Announce the Topic/Purpose: (what you want your audience to believe/do; 1-2 sentences)

    C. Motivate Listening: (briefly state relevance to your audience; why is this important to them?)

    D. Establish Your Credibility: (dynamism, competence, trustworthiness, appearance, experience, accolades, or a representative anecdote/story)

    E. Sign-Post the Main Points:

        1. Define "the issues" (consequences, size and relevance to your audience)

        2. Define/Address "the barriers" (what keeps your audience from resolving the issues?)

        3. Propose "the solutions" (do-able action steps you want your audience to take)

Transition sentence:

II. Body ("Tell 'em!")

    A. **The Issues**-State the problem or opportunity... magnitude, consequences/ rewards, relevance

        1. Provide statistical support to show magnitude/size of the issues

        2. Progressively develop 'consequences/rewards' and provide evidence of consequences and rewards of taking or not taking action.

            a. Harms and Benefits of taking/not taking action (provide examples)

            b. More Harmful and More Beneficial (provide examples)

Get A Klu, Inc.
PO Box 720891
San Diego CA 92172
Phone: 619-405-3456

Fax 740-539-2346
Email: info@getaklu.net
WEB: www.getaklu.net

17

Copyright 2018. Get A Klu, Inc. All Rights Reserved

      c. Most Harmful and Most Beneficial (provide examples, make emotional appeals!)

3. Use motivational appeals

      d. Emphasize "relevance" to your audience...interact with them if you are able!

      e. Get audience to imagine being 'harmed' by the problem or "rewarded" by the opportunity

4. Remember to stay credible, vulnerable, interactive and appealing to audience emotion!

Transition sentence:

B. **The Barriers**-Why doe the issue exist? What keeps it from being resolved?

1. There are two categories of Barriers to solving any problem or realizing any opportunity...they are:

      a. Structural Barriers-consists of laws, rules, codes, mandates, etc.

      b. Attitudinal Barriers-consists of people's opinions, beliefs, mindsets, values, or ignorance towards an issue/problem.

2. Provide a piece of Evidence for every Barrier

3. Evidence = Facts, Statistics, Stories, Testimonials, Analogies, Comparisons, etc.

Transition sentence:

Get A Klu, Inc.
PO Box 720491
San Diego CA 92172
Phone 619-405-9358

Fax 740-930-2346
Email: info@getaklu.net
WEB: www.getaklu.net

38

Copyright 2018 Get A Klu, Inc. All Rights Reserved

GET THEM TO TAKE ACTION! PLANNING
A PERSUASIVE/SALES PRESENTATION

    C. **The Solutions**-Propose specific actions steps using both logical and emotional appeal

        1. Solutions MUST include by your audience

        2. Solutions MUST be targeted at eliminating the barriers you've identified

        3. Solutions MUST be reasonable/do-able immediately!

Transition sentence:

III. **Conclusion** ("Tell 'em what you told 'em!" Quickly summarize and wrap up..."while they're hot!")

    A. **Restate your main points:**

        1. The Issues

        2. The Barriers

        3. The Solutions

    B. **Reason to Remember:** (can also phrase in terms of 'reason to get involved/ take action')

    C. **Visualize Solutions Working:** (evoke the imagination and emotion of your audience)

    D. **Tie-back:** to your introduction for a coherent ending!

Get A Klu, Inc.
PO Box 720891
San Diego CA 92172
Phone 619-405-3358

Fax 740-539-2346
Email info@getaklu.net
WEB: www.getaklu.net

39

Copyright 2018 Get A Klu, Inc. All Rights Reserved

WORK-LIFE BALANCE

T I P #1

THE BENEFITS OF BALANCE

The first step in achieving balance is to understand how important balance is. This is especially true for the entrepreneur/owner who is responsible for the success of one or more businesses and who has a tendency to allow that responsibility to be the reason they get out of balance!

Understanding the benefits of a healthy balanced life will motivate anyone to make necessary changes. Balance will improve the lives of individual employees, as well as the company culture. Learning the basics of work-life balance will also increase employee productivity, health, and morale.

Why It's Important

A healthy balance between work and home should be a priority for everyone. Implementing proper work-life balance offers many important benefits. There are, however, many hazards linked with an unbalanced work and home life.

Risks

- **Poor health:** Working long hours without taking time to relax will take its toll on health.
- **Unresolved conflict:** A lack of balance can create conflicts at work and at home.
- **Poor performance:** Taking on too much responsibility will lead to exhaustion and cause performance to suffer.

- **Financial loss:** The impact on health and productivity takes a financial toll on both individual employees and organizations.

Benefits

- **Fulfillment:** People who successfully implement work-life balance improve their sense of fulfillment at work and at home.
- **Health:** A healthy work-life balance decreases the risk of heart disease and other health problems.
- **Greater productivity:** Being relaxed and well rested increases productivity and improves work performance.
- **Stronger relationships:** Personal and professional relationships are strengthened, and conflicts are avoided when there is work-life balance.

Increased Productivity

 While it may seem counterintuitive, work-life balance can actually increase productivity. While it is true that overtime will initially increase production, the surge only lasts a few weeks before taking a destructive toll on productivity. In fact, working long hours for an extended time period will lead to exhaustion and unhealthy habits that decrease productivity.

Shorter work hours will actually increase productivity in the long-term. Additionally, studies show that people who take short, frequent breaks are more productive than people who only take a single break or work all day. Most people recommend taking a few minutes each hour to regroup.

Ways to increase productivity:

- **Take healthy breaks:** You should take time to refresh yourself. Try stretching, walking, or meditating throughout the day. This will also improve your health and overall wellbeing.
- **Take enjoyable breaks:** A recent study by Don J.Q. Chen and Vivien K.G Lim of the National University of Singapore discovered that taking a few moments to surf the Internet and mentally change gears actually

increases productivity. This fun activity increases productivity by nine percent.

- **Take time off:** Working to the point of burnout is not productive or healthy. Do not lose vacation days, even if you have to spread them out. Studies show that people who take their vacations are much more productive than those who do not.

Improved Mental and Physical Health

It is common knowledge that stress is directly linked to different diseases. Numerous surveys have discovered that work is a leading cause of stress related illness and injury, such as stroke, heart disease, and mental breakdowns. A balanced life will improve both physical and mental health.

How to Improve Health

- **Awareness:** A balanced lifestyle increases personal awareness, allowing individuals to identify potential health problems early.
- **Lifestyle:** A balanced lifestyle automatically improves health. It encourages healthy choices and helps develop the body and the mind.

Increased Morale

Work-life balance is an effective tool for increasing morale and improving company culture. Employees seek out companies that support healthy work-life balance. The only factor more important than balance to job seekers is compensation.

According to several surveys, work-life balance improves happiness and overall job satisfaction. Additionally, employees are more invested in companies that support their work-life balance. Work-life balance typically translates to employees who work harder and are more productive.

T I P #2

READ THE SIGNS!

The signs of imbalance are unmistakable. We see people suffering from poor health, burnout, and stress every day. For companies, this increases absenteeism, health costs, and turnover. If you recognize these signs in your life or your organization, take action immediately and focus on work-life balance.

Health Risks

Imbalance promotes poor health. Over time, this can lead to devastating, and possibly life-changing consequences.

Effects on Health:

- **Obesity**: Not taking the time to exercise or eat well can increase obesity, which is connected to heart disease and numerous other health risks.

- **Exhaustion**: Sleeping well can add years to a person's life. Sacrificing sleep for work will have negative effects on health and increase the chances of getting sick.

- **Emotional problems**: Stress and exhaustion will wreak havoc on emotional well-being. This will affect relationships and personal identity.

More companies are taking an interest in the health and fitness of their employees. It is in an organization's best interest to do so. Healthy employees are productive, absent less, and their health care costs less.

Absenteeism

Poor health increases employee absenteeism and thus is a costly problem for employers. There are hidden and direct costs that must be paid when an employee is absent from work.

Cost of absenteeism:

- **Sick pay:** Employees with sick days are still paid, which is a direct cost.
- **Loss of productivity:** Even with someone to work the position of the sick employee, the employee familiar with the job will be more productive. This is an indirect cost of sick days.

While most people who take time off are legitimately sick, stressed employees will take days off to catch up with personal obligations, and they usually feel justified doing so.

Burnout

Most people know that overworked employees eventually burnout. Burnout is the physical and psychological response to long-term stress.

Signs of Burnout:

- **Loss of interest:** Burned-out employees cannot make themselves care about their work, which is the source of their stress.
- **Lack of emotion:** Emotional responses are abnormal when someone is burned out.
- **Loss of motivation:** Former motivators no longer are effective.
- **Possible depression:** Burnout is closely linked to depression.

Burnout harms companies by increasing turnover. Consider the following:

- When everything is added together, 150 percent of an employee's annual salary is the cost of turnover.
- This number is 200 to 250 percent for members of management.

Stress

Work is the main source of stress for most Americans. Stress's connection to obesity for workers in sedentary jobs is more significant than diet, according to research published in the *Journal of Occupational and Environmental Medicine*. The effects stress has on heart health can be deadly.

Signs of Stress:

- **Overemotional**: People under stress can find it difficult to control their emotions.
- **Lethargy**: The physiological impact of stress can cause lethargy.
- **Restlessness:** Stress can make it difficult to focus, causing hyperactivity and restlessness.
- **Anxiety:** Prolonged stress can cause anxiety disorders.

> Vipul and I are not shy about sharing our stories of being out of balance and the harm it can cause. I can think of three or four times in my life when I was very much out of balance in both directions—sometimes, over-committed to a workplace, career, or business issue/objective and other times, ignoring professional obligations or opportunities from being over committed to family or personal issues.
>
> It hurts to do it, but Vipul and I are happy to share real stories of regret from imbalance that we hope to help you avoid! Looking forward to seeing you at our weekly tip reading!

T I P #3

RESOURCES FOR YOUR(SELF) EMPLOYEES

This tip is written to the entrepreneur/owner seeking to provide work-life balance for her/his employees. We encourage you to apply these suggestions to yourself ... consider your own work-life balance as the model and guide for what you provide to your employees!

Employers have the opportunity to improve work-life balance for their employees and increase productivity at the same time. Using the resources that employers have at their disposal to change work conditions may seem counterproductive, but they are effective.

Offer More Employee Control

Traditionally, employers set all of the parameters concerning jobs. Keeping all of the control, however, augments stress on employees. Simply offering employees more control over their lives and establishing better work-life balance will help alleviate this stress. Studies show that employee control actually increases loyalty and productivity.

Ways to offer control include flex time, job sharing, and, my favorite, telecommuting. Anything that empowers an employee to take charge of his or her life offers employee control.

Ask Employees for Suggestions

Employees have some of the best ideas on how to improve their jobs and the company as a whole. These ideas, however, are not always communicated. Many employees do not feel that people in management care, and most managers do not have the time to sit down with each employee. The best way to hear about new, innovative ideas is to create an employee suggestion program.

Tips:

- **Make it simple:** Create a simple process for giving suggestions; complicated rules do not encourage creativity.
- **Respond:** Let employees know that you have their suggestions and will consider them.
- **Thank:** Thank each employee who gives a suggestion, even if they are suggestions you do not use.
- **Reward:** Employees who come up with useful suggestions need to be rewarded.

Employee Assistance Program (EAP)

 Given the unavoidable stress of life, most people face times when they need assistance. EAPs provide employees access to counseling and other services. Without the aid of EAP counselors, the effects of stress can spiral out of control. Employee assistance programs give individuals the opportunity to seek help and learn the skills necessary to improve their work-life balance.

Typical EAP Topics:

- Personal crisis
- Work stress
- Finances
- Substances

EAPs are useful investments because they prevent turnover and reduce absences as they teach strategies for work-life balance.

Reward Your Staff

This may seem basic, but rewarding your staff is an effective method for promoting work-life balance. Employees who feel appreciated are more confident, and rewards reinforce the behavior you want to see repeated. Rewards can also provide breaks that reduce stress. Rewards do not have to break the bank. There are simple ways to thank your employees for their service.

Useful Rewards: Some of our favorites include public acknowledgement of service, extra time off, awards/bonuses, promotions, and parties!

Vipul and I look forward to learning about work-life balance resources that you are aware of not mentioned here. Please make plans to join our live tip reading on this tip/topic!

T I P #4

STOP CALLING IT "TIME MANAGEMENT"

 This tip also makes an appearance in the second edition of *Get A Klu in 52*, but in the Accountability section!

The number one strategy for time management is to set goals. If you do a great job with goal setting, you will make better decisions about what you do "in time."

We teach S.M.A.A.R.T. goal setting (also its own tip in the Accountability section of the first edition of *Get A Klu in 52*). And we go really deep and thorough on the psychology of goal setting, including why people fail to set goals and how to make sure both motivation and accountability are built into the goal-setting process. For now, let us be clear that there is NO GREATER strategy for "time management" than rigorous and disciplined S.M.A.A.R.T. goal setting!

Beyond that, you need to STOP calling it "time management" for some very important reasons.

- Time manages itself ... quite well, in fact. I encourage you to read a book by a future friend of mine, Mitch Albom, called *The Timekeeper*. The book is about a curse bestowed upon the first person to ever attempt to measure (control/manage) time. It is a tremendous read that will change your perspectives on time altogether. My suggestion is to simply be humble and honest and admit that we do not manage time—time is a concept far beyond us and totally automated with no help from us.

- Second, what CAN we manage? Ourselves! Our moods, our decisions, our actions, all of which occur in time, but can you see how the focus shifts toward accountability when we get honest about what we truly CAN manage? I love public speaking on this topic when I ask people to repeat after me if they have ever said out loud the things I say out loud, like, "I don't have time"... "If only there were more time"... "I ran out of time"... "I don't have self"...gotcha! You never say that last one! "If only there were more tasks"... "I ran out of purpose"... "If only there were more discipline in the day"... do you see what I'm getting at? When we look within at what we CAN control, we can be accountable ... so most people call it time management as if it is the fault of time that we are underachieving.

- Finally, when we say, "I need better time management," we have a victim mindset. Were we to say instead, "I need better decision management or self-management—or task management—or calendar management—or purpose/priority management," we would be demonstrating an "accountable mindset." Stay accountable, my friends!

Now that you are calling it SOMETHING more accurate and accountable, here are some basic tips we can offer to do a better job at it!

Understand the Urgent/Important Matrix

Many people confuse the urgent with the important. Urgent tasks do need to be done quickly, but that does not make them important. We are often stuck completing urgent tasks at the expense of the important ones. Important tasks are the ones that help us meet goals.

Often, urgent tasks, such as fixing the copy machine, are distractions from what is important. Learning the difference between urgent and important will better anyone's time management skills.

The matrix on the next page explains the difference between urgent and important. Understanding it can help you identify the tasks that will help you meet your goals.

The Urgent / Important Matrix

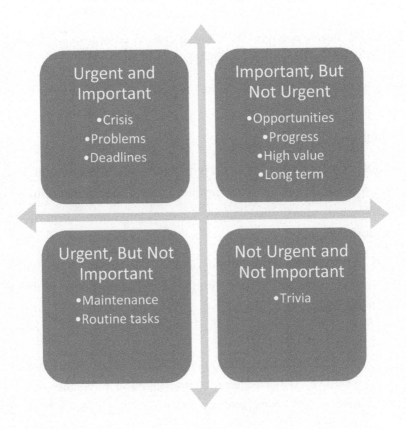

Urgent and Important
- Crisis
- Problems
- Deadlines

Important, But Not Urgent
- Opportunities
- Progress
- High value
- Long term

Urgent, But Not Important
- Maintenance
- Routine tasks

Not Urgent and Not Important
- Trivia

Learn to Say No

Managing time requires that people learn to say "no." This may seem cruel, but it is not possible to meet everyone's needs. You must learn to say "no" kindly but firmly.

Do not allow people to talk you into urgent tasks. You need to stick with a schedule and plan of action. Do not deviate unless it is a true emergency. For example, proofing a colleague's letter is not an emergency that you must complete at once. Complete your important tasks first.

Stay Flexible

Flexibility is an important skill. Life cannot be predicted, and inflexible people fall to pieces when change beyond their control comes. Being flexible simply means that you are not resisting the inevitable changes of life.

Flexibility is not passivity. It is being able to embrace change. This will reduce stress and improve work-life balance.

For example, car trouble will throw off your schedule, so do not try to keep up with your tasks that day.

80/20 Rule

According to the 80/20 rule, 80 percent of our success is the result of only 20 percent of our actions. The rule implies that we should place our focus on the 20 percent of activities that are the most successful. This requires that we prioritize goals.

When this is done, concentrate on the 20 percent of activities that aggressively move you toward those goals. Give most of your attention to this 20 percent.

> In our coaching and leadership trainings, Vipul and I teach more extensive "self-management" strategies and techniques. We have lots of habits, practices, exercises to help you literally master your calendar. Our goal in that training is to put you in a position to help others master their calendars. It starts with self-mastery, not "time management!"

T I P #5

PRO-VENTIONAL WAYS TO WORK!

 As of this writing, the world is struggling to emerge from COVID-era shifts to virtual work at a pace well beyond what we were seeing prior to the pandemic. Suffice it say, "conventional" ways of working have been challenged like never before, and it's healthy to look for "pro-ventional" ways of working that promote work-life balance for self and staff.

By the way, hats off to our very good friend and Inner Business Coach, Patty Blakesley, with whom I brainstormed the idea of replacing "con" with "pro" in certain words. We associate the word "con" with negative, while "pro" is what we associate with positive. Patty and I came up with this when discussing the ability of a world-class coach to confront clients with accountability. Some people naturally "avoid" confrontation, so we decided to call it PROfrontation to make it more desirable to do neurolinguisticly!

Likewise, here in Tip #5, we encourage you to find "PROventional" ways of working for yourself and employees that facilitate work-life balance.

We briefly mentioned some of these "resources" in an earlier tip in this section but are ready to elaborate in this tip.

> **KLOOBY SNACK**
>
> It's healthy to look for "PRO-ventional ways of working that promote work-life balance for self and staff.

Optional Ways to Work

The traditional methods of work may increase stress and imbalance in life. Each person is unique and providing different work options will allow people to choose the method that helps them be their most productive and maintain their balance. While it may not be possible to provide every option, allowing for different work styles will improve company culture and promote balance. Each option comes with its own pros and cons, so examine them carefully before choosing a new way to work.

Telecommuting

Given the way we use technology, telecommuting is a popular work option. This allows people to work from home and send their projects in when they are due.

Pros:

- **Cost:** Companies can reduce overhead and other costs by allowing employees to work from home.
- **Productivity:** People who work from home are often more productive.
- **Lowers stress:** Many employees benefit from losing morning commutes and distracting office mates.
- **Personal control:** Employees who work from home are able to take responsibility for their own schedules.

Cons:

- **Communication:** When all communication is electronic, employees may not communicate as well as they can face-to-face. Additionally, a lack of social interaction can isolate employees and stunt company culture.
- **Motivation:** People who are not self-driven are not successful and need more accountability than telecommuting offers.

- **Longer hours:** Some people work longer hours when they telecommute because there is no distinction between work and home.

Job Sharing

Job sharing is a popular option that allows employees to balance their work and home lives. This technique allows two people to share a job, with each one working part-time hours.

Pros:

- **Better attendance:** When people have the time to handle personal matters, they are less likely to miss work.
- **Continuity:** With two people sharing a job, there is always someone to come in and cover for a sick employee.
- **Morale:** Employees who are able to find work-life balance have better morale and productivity.

Cons:

- **Conflict:** People who want to be in control may not enjoy having an equal share their responsibilities. This can cause conflicts between job sharers.
- **Inequality:** If one employee is more effective than the other, that employee may shoulder too much responsibility.
- **More paperwork:** Employers have to double the paperwork for shared jobs.

Job Redesign

Sometimes it is necessary to redesign a position to alleviate stress. This requires analyzing and changing the scope and responsibilities of a position in a way that will motivate employees and improve their work-life balance.

The method:

- Content: Discover what information leads to problems at work.
- Information: Analyze job information to find inconsistencies.

- Elements: Change the elements of the job.
- Description: Rewrite the job description.
- Responsibilities: Refocus responsibilities based on the description.

Flex Time

Flex time does not alter the number of hours employees work, but it does give them the flexibility to choose when they work. For example, an employee may choose to come at 7:00 am and leave at 4:00 pm to spend time with family.

Pros:

- **Productivity:** People are more productive when they know they will be able to take care of their other obligations.
- **Morale:** Everyone's internal clock is different. People are happier when they can work at their optimal times.

Cons:

- **Difficult to manage:** Managers may have trouble coordinating meetings when everyone works different hours.
- **Miscommunications**: It is easy to forget to communicate ideas with people who have already left for the day.

Vipul and I hope this got your wheels spinning on possibilities for adjusting the ways you or your people conduct their work so as to promote work-life balance. And we look forward to learning about more options for conducting work that we may not have covered here. Please consider emailing us with your ideas/ experiences: info@getaklu.net or joining us live online when we discuss this specific tip in 2022!

T I P #6

BE PRESENT AT WORK

 Keeping balance when at work is difficult. Outside influences always try to creep in and destroy productivity. Becoming sidetracked, however, simply creates job-related stress that further increases the level of imbalance you experience.

Fortunately, there are a few useful tips that will help you regain your sense of balance while at work.

Leave Home Stress at Home

Everyone has personal problems that create stress and hinder job performance. If these issues are severe, it may be necessary to take a leave of absence. In most cases, however, there are better strategies to help leave the home stress at home.

Strategies:

- **Get up early**: Get up early enough to take a few minutes and prepare for a new day. Focus on what is ahead, not the past.
- **Take advantage of the commute:** View the commute as a chance to enter your "work zone." That is, mentally gear up for the workday.
- **Communicate appropriately:** Discuss your problems with a friend or confidant outside of work. Do not vent about home stress to your coworkers.
- **Find outlets:** Discover useful ways to alleviate stress, such as exercise. This will help keep you focused throughout the workday.

Break Up Large Tasks

Projects and deadlines can be overwhelming. If you have a large task ahead of you, you might be tempted to procrastinate. This will only create more stress. A better solution is breaking up the task.

Tips:

- List the steps that are necessary to complete the task.
- Schedule time for each step.
- Complete the easiest step first, and then move on to the next easiest. This will give you a sense of accomplishment.
- Do not look ahead. Focus on the task at hand.

Delegate

People can avoid stress by simply delegating responsibility. This sounds simple, but many people, particularly those in management, have problems delegating authority. They do not trust others to do the job. There are a few tips that will help anyone feel more confident about delegating.

Steps:

- **Choose tasks to delegate:** Do not delegate sensitive or difficult tasks.
- **Choose people to help:** Find responsible people you trust to handle the tasks for you.
- **Give instructions**: Make sure you communicate clear instructions with deadlines.
- **Be available**: Let people know that they can come to you with questions, but do not hover over them.

(Once Again) Set Accurate S.M.A.A.R.T. Goals

Accurate goals decrease stress. This involves estimating the time that it will take to complete something. There are a few steps that will help you set accurate goals.

Steps:

- Familiarize yourself with the requirements.
- List the actions that need to happen.
- Estimate the time necessary for each action you need to take.
- Estimate the total time necessary for a task.

Mindset Coaching (or other assistance)

A difficult truth to accept is that none of the suggestions in this tip will work without mindset skills that can be acquired through coaching or other professional assistance. I always like to say, *"It isn't a good idea to build a mansion on top of quicksand!"* Your mindset and the ability to author (determine, choose, select, create) any state of mind you wish at any time is the most important ability we recommend you acquire.

KLOOBY SNACK

It isn't a good idea to build a mansion on top of quicksand!

While we only touch on "mindset" here, we fully teach and train on it inside of our Coaching and Leadership Training. When you learn how to author your state of mind and help others to do the same, you are well on your way to greater work-life balance!

TIP #7

BE PRESENT AT HOME WHEN AT HOME

We should be able to relax at home and unwind after a hard day at work. Unfortunately, this does not always happen. Home has stress of its own, and it seems like the stress from work is constantly waiting to spill over into our home lives. To have work-life balance, it is important to learn how to effectively manage the stress and obligations at home.

Leave Work Stress at Work

Bringing the stress of work home will ruin your family life. Additionally, not being able to separate from work will destroy your balance, increasing your stress level. Luckily, there are a few strategies that will help keep work separate.

Strategies:

- **Stop on the way home:** On particularly stressful days, you may want to stop somewhere for a few minutes and decompress.
- **Vent in the car or to a friend:** Use the daily traffic jam as a chance to express your frustrations to yourself, instead of ranting about them to your family.
- **Enjoy your family:** Do not focus on the downside of family life. Find ways to spend time together that everyone enjoys.
- **Find outlets:** Discover useful ways to alleviate work stress, such as exercise or meditation. Practicing these will help you focus on the present.

Turn Your Phone Off

Cell phones have made it nearly impossible to escape the pressures of life. Now there is always a way for someone to reach us. Not only are we inundated with phone calls, we have emails and social networks to worry about. There is only one way to fix the problem and alleviate stress: TURN OFF THE PHONE. It is acceptable and healthy to occasionally disconnect. It doesn't matter when you disconnect, just that you do. (Silencing the phone does not count as disconnecting.)

Take Some "Me" Time

"Me time" is essential to a person's health and wellbeing. Often, people think that "me time" is a day at the spa or something extravagant that they can't afford to do. Actually, "me time" is much simpler. It is anything that you do just for yourself. There is no set expense or time frame that you have to follow when taking "me time." It can be as simple as taking a walk. The only imperative concerning "me time" is that you actually take it.

Maintain Your Boundaries

Boundaries are important in every aspect of life. Without them, people will constantly pull our attention away from what is important.

In order to achieve work-life balance, it is necessary to establish boundaries between work and home. This will require you to determine what those boundaries are and communicate them. For example, you may set a boundary that says you do not take calls after 7:00 pm. Each person's boundaries will be different, so think about what works for you.

Once you set your boundaries and communicate them, you need to maintain them. People naturally push boundaries, and they will test you. You need to stay strong. For example, let a call go to voicemail and only return it if the matter is truly an emergency that cannot wait. Odds are it is not. After time, other people will learn to respect your boundaries.

T I P #8

STOP CALLING IT "STRESS MANAGEMENT"

 Why not call it "Wellness Welcoming" … or something? What we mean is to avoid giving any "life" to stress at all. As soon as we say we want to manage stress, our mindset is almost ensuring that we always have some. The first suggestion we have when it comes to "stress management" is to find a positive way of referring to it—a term we really like is "self-care" because it says that we truly want: to take responsibility of caring for ourselves!

Having said that (we really do prefer that you refer to this topic as "self-care" instead of "stress management"), we must acknowledge, without giving it more life/attention/power than it deserves, that at least some stress is unavoidable, and some levels of stress are actually healthy. Some stress can motivate action, creative problem-solving, adaptability, and other positive outcomes.

> **KLOOBY SNACK**
> Self-care is not too complicated to understand … it is learning to prioritize self-care that is harder to teach!

Yet if we do not handle stress well when it naturally shows up, it grows beyond a healthy motivator into something that can cause lasting physical and psychological damage. All the while, effective and consistent self-care can combat the negative effects of stress. Fortunately, self-care is not too complicated to understand … we believe anyone can learn how to care for themselves … it is learning to prioritize self-care that is harder to teach!

Here are the most basic suggestions for self-care. In our weekly tip reading online or in private coaching with you, we can go deeper or broader on the myriad strategies/options when it comes to self-care.

Exercise

Everyone knows that exercise is an important part of a healthy lifestyle, but it is also a key aspect to managing stress. Exercise affects people mentally, as well as physically. It produces endorphins that will improve your mood and prevent depression. In order to reap the benefits of exercise, however, you must be consistent with it.

Tips for Success:

- **Choose an exercise you enjoy:** You will not repeat an activity that you hate doing.
- **Start slowly**: If you overdo it, you will simply become tired and discouraged.
- **Schedule it:** Exercise must be a priority, or you will never get to it.

Eating Well

Diet has a strong impact on our emotions and the way we handle stress. Eating well is an important factor in stress management.

Unfortunately, our bodies crave fatty, salty foods in times of stress. Rather than giving in to fast food cravings, focus on getting healthy.

Tips:

- **Avoid sugar and caffeine:** Their highs may give you more energy, but once you crash, you are left more exhausted than before.
- **Focus on nutrition:** Be sure to include whole grains, lean protein, and leafy greens in your diet.
- **Eat frequently:** Increase your focus by eating small healthy snacks throughout the day. This will balance blood sugar and increase energy.

Getting Enough Sleep

Many people are sleep deprived. Experts recommend sleeping between seven and nine hours a night. Sleep deprivation increases stress, weakens the immune system, and raises the risk of accidents. Given the important role that sleeps plays in physical and mental health, it only makes sense to do everything in your power to improve sleep.

Ways to Improve Sleep

- **Avoid electronics before bed:** Studies show that the light of the television, phone, or computer may make falling asleep difficult.
- **Relax:** Unwind with a relaxing routine before bed.
- **Exercise:** Exercise will make it easier to fall asleep.
- **Have a bedtime:** A regular bedtime will train your body's internal clock and help you fall asleep.

Self-Assessment

We are not always aware of how much stress is affecting our lives. It is possible to believe that you are effectively managing your stress when, in reality, stress is managing you. This is why it is important to step back and assess your stress level. The results of the assessment will reveal any changes that you need to make in order to improve your stress management. You can use the results of the assessment to make the necessary changes to your diet, exercise, and sleep routines.

Worksheet: Self-Assessment: Choose the appropriate number for each statement!

1 = Always, 2 = Sometimes, 3 = Never

1. I oversleep.

   1   2   3

2. I feel tired throughout the day.

   1   2   3

3. I crave junk food at work.

   1 2 3

4. I forget to exercise.

   1 2 3

5. I eat fast food.

   1 2 3

6. I catch illnesses easily.

   1 2 3

7. I suffer from headaches.

   1 2 3

8. I have trouble falling asleep.

   1 2 3

9. I think I need to lose weight.

   1 2 3

10. I think about work when I should be sleeping.

   1 2 3

Score:

10-14 = Stressed: You need to take steps to manage your stress now.

15-20 = Slightly stressed: You could make improvements to your stress management.

21-30 = Managing: You are pretty well balanced. Keep monitoring your stress.

If you are being honest and didn't like your score, please consider scheduling two complimentary sessions with Vipul and myself so we can help you pinpoint sources and remedies for unwanted stress.

T I P #9

THERE'S NO PLACE LIKE (working from) HOME

Working from home has its advantages and disadvantages. Working in a home office and maintaining work-life balance requires preparation and regular evaluation of your work practices. This has never been more challenging than during the pandemic that we are living in as of the writing of this book.

If we are not careful, our home offices can take over our lives. By following a few guidelines, we can avoid burnout as we take advantage of the many benefits of working at home.

Setting Up a Home Office

It is important to set up the home office properly in the beginning. A poor work environment will only harm productivity. So, make sure that you are comfortable and have all of the tools that you need to do your job well.

The Set Up:

- **Location:** Choose a separate room or a location that is out of the way. This will help prevent distractions and create a professional work environment. You also need to make sure it is well lit.

- **Equipment:** Make sure your equipment is functional and you have everything you need.

- **Clear out the office:** Remove items from the office that are not work related. It is not a storage shed.

- **Organize:** Organize supplies so they are accessible, easy to use, and functional.

- **Make it a workspace:** Limit the office use for work. It is not a play area.

Setting Boundaries

It is difficult to establish boundaries in a home office; people do not view a home the same way they see the work office. Because you do not have company policies to prevent distractions, you need to create your own boundaries. You can base these boundaries on the rules and boundaries of your old workplace. For example, do not take personal calls while you are working. Just like other boundaries, expect people to challenge them. You must stick to your boundaries, however, in order to be effective at your job and keep your work and life in balance.

Dealing with Distractions

It is easy to become distracted while working from home. There is no one to supervise, and your family can easily forget that you are working. Fortunately, a few safeguards will help you avoid distractions.

Avoiding Distractions:

- **Limit access:** Ask your family to stay out of the office while you are working. Family, children especially, can be very distracting.

- **Use a timer:** Schedule breaks for activities like social networking. Do not constantly surf the Internet.

- **Turn off the television:** Even if you need a television for work, it does not have to be on all the time. Turn it off to avoid distractions.

- **Set aside time to talk on the phone:** You cannot allow yourself to be distracted by every phone call.

Make a Schedule and Stick to It

Working from home gives you the chance to create your own schedule, but you do need to create it. If not, you will have trouble accomplishing tasks on time. Most people find a schedule that sets tasks for each hour helpful, but you may use any format or time block you like.

Example:

- 8:00 am – Breakfast
- 8:30 am – Return emails
- 9:00 am – Call clients
- 10:00 am – Research

No matter how you create your schedule, you must stick with it. It is too easy to ignore your schedule when no one is monitoring your performance.

Vipul and I absolutely LOVE to talk about calendar and schedule management strategies, whether we are talking about working from home or not. The habit of actively managing your schedule, especially the critical "appointments with self" that we need to attend, with punctuality and discipline will really help us make the most of working from home ... whether we have chosen or are forced to work from home, we really believe these suggestions will help!

T I P #10

WHEN BALANCE IS B.S.!

 Vipul and I would like to begin this tip with a shout out to our mutual friend, Maresa Friedman. She is an amazing marketing strategist, the founder of Executive Cat Herder, and one of the most brilliant women I have ever met or worked with.

Maresa told me she drafted a book called, *Balance is B_ _ _ S_ _ _!*, where she offered some arguments that are counter to what we normally hear about balance. The first nine tips in this section are things you might normally hear ... balance is good, critical for our health, necessary for a fulfilling life, be present, practice self-care, etc.

Maresa calls B.S. on all of that just long enough to argue FOR the hustle, the grind, the pursuit of any sort of greatness or worthwhile achievement that requires sacrifice and a little imbalance.

Vipul and I agree. If you want to be great at something, if you want to achieve something great, if you want great results in one area of your life, you might have to make sacrifices in other areas in order to get them.

Balance can always be restored from imbalance. The tips in this section are not to suggest that you must always be "in balance" or that you must always strive to be or stay "in balance." These tips are to help you FIND balance if it has been lost ... to help you minimize the effects of imbalance when you are pushing for something great!

Remember, we spent the first 42 tips of this book showing you how hard you'll have to work to be the entrepreneur/business owner that you want to be. It is only fair that we invest 10 tips in helping you restore balance among the 12- to 18-hour workdays you have or will, no doubt, become accustomed to on your journey as an entrepreneur!

T I P #11

HIRE A COACH!

Vipul and I believe that the best way to achieve any balance in work, in life, or in both is to get help when you need it. Maybe there is simply too much on your plate or you need support, guidance, or expertise in a particular area. This is especially true for business owners and entrepreneurs, who tend to want to "do it all," even when they admit that they don't know it all.

This book provides tips to help you build the soft skills that strong leaders need, but they're tips—the condensed bullet -point version of the in-depth coaching and training we provide to our clients. Not only do we expand on these tips in our coaching sessions, but you'll find we also have an arsenal of additional tips to share with you.

Fittingly, the last tip in this book is to hire a coach. We don't care if it's us— we just know everybody's life and business will be better when they have external coaching.

That said, we actually do hope the coach you hire IS us! We absolutely love helping businesses! We love helping entrepreneurs, and we love helping people grow. And when it comes to work-life balance, we've got you covered.

A word about coaches: some coaches are great life coaches, and some coaches are great business coaches. Some coaches get more specific within either of those two categories, such as fitness, nutrition, or relationships. On the business side, there is sales coaching, marketing coaching, leadership coaching, and even motivational coaching. In this book, Vipul and I have attempted to show you that the combination of his business acumen and my master's degree in communication gives us the coverage to help most people better than most coaches can — at least we think so!

Throughout this book we've mentioned that we are offering two complementary sessions with either me or Vipul, or both of us — or coaches we have trained, if they are a better fit. As long as you haven't taken advantage of our offer and experienced those complementary sessions already, they are yours for the taking ... and we do hope you take them!

Finally, it is absolutely free to join our weekly Zooms that we will stream into our social media channels. In these Zooms, we discuss one tip from this book every week and share our personal stories and elaborate on each tip throughout the year. After we discuss each tip, there is always free group coaching waiting for you, as well — not to mention the networking and relationship building that will come from the environment Vipul and I believe we can successfully create!

Through these offerings, you have many more opportunities to "Get a Klu" in the next year!

> Vipul and I hope we have validated or assisted you wherever you are along the entrepreneur's journey. We hope this collection of 52 tips ending with these 11 for work-life balance provide value and is worth sharing or recommending. We certainly look forward to discussing these tips with you in our weekly live sessions OR privately in the two complimentary sessions we keep offering you!
>
> Above all, we want to thank you for investing in this book and for any feedback you have as to how we can improve it for future editions that are better than this, the first "Entrepreneur's Edition" of Get A Klu in 52! Thank you so much!

ABOUT JEFFREY KLUBECK

At the intersection of academia and business, Jeffrey Klubeck has applied his Master's Degree in Communication to over 20 years of experience in organizational development and transformational business coaching. A coach before it was the trend, Jeffrey has had the opportunity to create performance management and talent recruitment frameworks with organizations such as JP Morgan Chase, State Farm, DOW Pharmaceutical, and King Pharmaceuticals.

With more than 3,000 learners and clients who have actively packed his courses in public speaking, interpersonal, and group communication, Jeff's experience as a former Professor of Communication has created a following of students and coaches who have been able to apply strategic critical thinking and paradigm shifts in their organizations.

Jeffrey has had the pleasure of speaking on 4 continents to audiences from over 40 countries. Jeffrey's teaching, training, and coaching programs have been game changing in helping executives, entrepreneurs, and business teams increase their motivation, accountability, and results!

Discover more at:

www.getaklu.net and www.theklubrary.com

ABOUT VIPUL DAYAL

Vipul Dayal is a "serial go-giver" who is constantly moving forward as an entrepreneur, philanthropist, speaker, author, community leader, proud husband and father of three! Vipul's hospitality development and management company, VNR Management, Inc., has operated his family-owned hotel businesses since 2009. Together with his wife, Reena, as franchise owner, Vipul opened his 15th business in San Diego, taking over the 4S Ranch location for Primrose Schools and providing accredited early education and care education to infants through kindergarten, after-schoolers, their families, and communities!

Vipul loves helping children and young professionals!

In 2012, Vipul was recognized by the County of San Diego as a Young Professional of the Month, and in 2014, Vipul's charitable work earned him AAHOA's (Asian American Hotel Owners Association) Outreach Award for Philanthropy. In, 2015, San Diego Metro recognized Vipul as one of San Diego's Top Men who Make a Difference, and in 2016, Vipul was included in the Top 20 Movers and Shakers by SD Metro.